Pocket Accountant

D0727995

The Economist

PUBLICATIONS

Pocket Accountant

Christopher Nobes

Basil Blackwell

and

The Economist Publications

LIBRARY
MARY BALDWIN COLLEGE

© Christopher Nobes

Jointly published 1985
Reprinted and first published in paperback 1987
Basil Blackwell Ltd
108 Cowley Road, Oxford OX4 1JF, UK
and *The Economist Publications*
40 Duke Street,
London W1A 1DW.

All rights reserved. Except for the quotation of short passages for the purposes of criticism and review, no part of this publication may be reproduced, stored in a retrieval system, or transmitted, in any form or by any means, electronic, mechanical, photocopying, recording or otherwise, without the prior permission of the publisher.

Except in the United States of America, this book is sold subject to the condition that it shall not, by way of trade or otherwise, be lent, re-sold, hired out, or otherwise circulated without the publisher's prior consent in any form of binding or cover other than that in which it is published and without a similar condition including this condition being imposed on the subsequent purchaser.

All the information in this book is verified to the best of the author's and publisher's ability, but they do not accept responsibility for loss arising from decisions based upon them. Where opinion is expressed it is that of the author, which does not necessarily coincide with the editorial views of The Economist Newspaper.

British Library Cataloguing in Publication Data

Nobes, C. W.
    The Economist pocket accountant.
    1. Accounting
    I. Title
    657   HF5635

ISBN 0-631-15592-9

Typeset by Getset (BTS) Ltd., Eynsham, Oxford
Printed in Gt. Britain by Billings, Worcester

JUN 2 3 1988

Contents

Dedication

To my surviving three forebears:
Beryl and Harold Nobes, and William Ramsey.

I would send her . . . to a boarding-school, in order to learn a little ingenuity and artifice. Then, Sir, she should have a supercilious knowledge of accounts; and as she grew up, I would have her instructed in geometry, that she might know something of the contagious countries.

Mrs Malaprop's views on education, including that in accounting.
R B Sheridan, The Rivals, Act I, Scene II

Preface

Accounting is a very ancient art which played a key role in the development of writing and numbers. As commerce and government have become more complicated, accounting has kept pace alongside, oiling the wheels of economic progress. The first book with a substantial treatise on double entry was published in 1494 in Venice. One of Goethe's characters called double entry "one of the fairest inventions of the human mind": it usually appeals to those who like algebra, *Times* crosswords or Bach cello suites!

Thus accounting is no confused parvenu like economics, nor ramshackle "ass" like the law. However, neither is it a science: there remains much judgment in accounting and, consequently, much controversy. This book is intended to be a guide to the jargon, the concepts and the uncertainties of accounting. Its basic context is the UK, but there are very frequent references and headings concerning the USA. In the case of many entries, knowledge of other entries is relevant; this is denoted by SMALL CAPITALS which indicate a cross-reference. For beginners, initial reference to some fundamental entries listed on the following page may be useful. There is also a list of abbreviations at the end of the book. The world of accounting is changing very fast, and the currency of this book will be affected by changes after mid-1984.*

My thanks are due to my colleagues Bob Parker and Bill McInnes for hundreds of helpful comments; to Susanne Robertson for the use of great word processing skill; to the Editor of *Accountancy* for permission to reprint the cartoons in the text; and to Sue Corbett and her colleagues at Basil Blackwell and *The Economist* for much help along the way.

Christopher Nobes
San Diego, November 1986

*Updated at the end of 1986.

Crash Course for Beginners

Those unfamiliar with accounting may like to begin by reading the following basic headings:

    Accountancy profession
    Accounting principles
    Accounting standards
    Accounts
    Asset
    Auditing
    Balance sheet
    Companies
    Conservatism
    Consolidated financial statements
    Depreciation
    Historical cost accounting
    Matching
    Materiality
    Profit and loss account
    True and fair view

Readers may also wish to consult other works by the author for more detailed treatment of:

(i)   basic financial accounting:

      C W Nobes, *Introduction to Financial Accounting*,
      Allen and Unwin, 1984

(ii) taxation:

      S R James and C W Nobes, *The Economics of Taxation*,
      Philip Allan, 1983

(iii) comparisons with other countries:
      C W Nobes and R H Parker, *Comparative International Accounting*,
      Philip Allan, 1985

(iv) accountancy firms, institutes and courses:
C W Nobes, *Becoming an Accountant*,
Longman, 1983

A

Above the line. – an expression relating to the income statement or profit and loss account. The 'line' in question is the 'net profit' or 'net income' of such statements. A '*below* the line' amount is an EXTRA-ORDINARY ITEM or an appropriation like dividends. Thus, an '*above* the line' amount is a normal expense or revenue of the business. Managements sometimes try to put as many expenses as possible below the line in order to improve the appearance of profit. EARNINGS PER SHARE figures are calculated excluding below the line amounts. It is the ACCOUNTING STANDARD on extraordinary items which attempts to 'hold the line' in this area. One Technical Partner in a multinational firm of accountants has suggested that the only workable standard would be one that said that all expenses were below the line and all revenues were above it!

Absorption costing. – the allocation of all fixed and VARIABLE COSTS in the calculation of the cost of goods or services produced. The opposite of this would be variable costing.

Accelerated depreciation. – DEPRECIATION at a faster rate than would be suggested by an asset's expected life. This is most commonly found in the context of tax concessions designed to encourage investment. For the calculation of taxable income in such cases, businesses would be allowed to depreciate certain assets (like energy-saving devices or assets in depressed regions) more quickly than accountants otherwise would. This occurs in many countries; for the UK system, see CAPITAL ALLOWANCES.

Accepting house. – a British financial institution that buys BILLS OF EXCHANGE from companies who would prefer to accept less cash now rather than the full cash amount later. A bill 'accepted' by the bank has that institution's backing. Thus, even the Bank of England would buy such an accepted bill. The Accepting Houses Committee comprises the seventeen top accepting houses in London.

Accountability. – the major original purpose of accounting; so that the owners of resources (now shareholders, for example) can check up on the managers or stewards of those resources (now boards of directors, for example). See STEWARDSHIP for a more detailed entry.

Accountancy profession. Accountancy is an exceptionally old occupation. However, the oldest professional bodies of accountants were formed in the 1850s in Edinburgh and Glasgow. Shortly afterwards, there was similar activity throughout the English-speaking world, and eventually elsewhere. The table illustrates this for some countries.

(For more detail on the UK bodies, see CONSULTATIVE COMMITTEE OF ACCOUNTANCY BODIES.)

The startling difference in the size of the professional bodies from country to country is partly because, for example, in Germany there is a separate profession of tax experts, the training period is longer, and only accountants in private practice may be members. However, there is a real difference in the number of companies to be audited, and the type of work in the audit. Perhaps the paucity of German accountants explains their country's 'economic miracle'!

The professional bodies set standards of entry for training; they operate training and examination systems; they make ethical rules; and,

Accountancy Bodies, Age and Membership

Country	Body	Founding Date*	Approx nos 000s
United States	American Institute of Certified Public Accountants	1887	200
Canada	Canadian Institute of Chartered Accountants	1902 (1880)	38
United Kingdom and Ireland**	Institute of Chartered Accountants in England and Wales	1880 (1870)	78
	Institute of Chartered Accountants of Scotland	1951 (1854)	11
	Chartered Association of Certified Accountants	1939 (1891)	26
	Institute of Chartered Accountants in Ireland	1888	5
Australia	Australian Society of Accountants	1952 (1887)	50
	Institute of Chartered Accountants in Australia	1928 (1886)	14
France	Ordre des Experts Comptables et des Comptables Agréés	1942	10
W Germany	Institut der Wirt-schaftsprüfer	1932	5
Netherlands	Nederlands Instituut van Registeraccountants	1895	5

*Dates in brackets are those of earliest predecessor bodies. **UK bodies are those whose members are allowed to audit companies.

'Same here — mine's a specialist in liquidation and receivership'

particularly in the Anglo-Saxon world, they set ACCOUNTING STAN-
DARDS and AUDITING STANDARDS.

The profession is also organized at an international level (see GROUPE
D'ETUDES, INTERNATIONAL FEDERATION OF ACCOUNTANTS). However, as
noted above, the profession differs substantially from country to
country. In FRANCE and WEST GERMANY, for example, there are both
private professional bodies of accountants and government controlled
bodies of auditors. Often the main method of entry to the latter is
membership of the former.

Accountants International Study Group (AISG). – a body founded
in 1966, comprising members from professional accountancy bodies in
the UK, the USA and Canada. Its purpose was to study and report on
accounting practices in the three countries. Twenty studies were issued,
mainly on financial reporting matters, for example on inventories
(1968), consolidated financial statements (1972) and interim reports
(1975). The AISG was wound up in 1977 when the INTERNATIONAL
FEDERATION OF ACCOUNTANTS was formed.

Account days. – the days on which dealers in stocks and shares have to
settle their bills. An account day is the end of an 'account period'. The
period varies from one Stock Exchange to another. In London, the year
is divided into twenty-four periods; in New York, one has to settle
within five days.

Accountancy and accounting. – These terms are used interchangeably
by many people. However, it tends to be, for example, the *accountancy*
profession, but management *accounting*. That is, the former tends to be
associated with the profession, and the latter with the subject matter,

particularly in the context of education or theory. Accounting includes mechanical aspects like DOUBLE ENTRY bookkeeping, which might be said to be part of financial accounting. The latter also involves the preparation, presentation and interpretation of financial statements. Then there is MANAGEMENT ACCOUNTING, which is more concerned with the use of accounting data for decision-making and control by managers.

Accounting conventions/concepts. – two of the expressions commonly used for the fundamental conceptual rules of accounting; see ACCOUNTING PRINCIPLES.

Accounting equation. – an algebraic representation of a summary of what happens in the DOUBLE ENTRY system. The BALANCE SHEET might be expressed as $A_0 = L_0 + C_0$ (i.e. total ASSETS at time zero = total LIABILITIES and CAPITAL at time zero). The capital figure grows from time zero to time one by the earning of profit for the period; that is $C_0 + P_1 = C_1$ (EQU 2). The profit (P_1) is made up of the total REVENUES less the total EXPENSES of the period; that is $P_1 = R_1 - E_1$ (EQU 3). It is, of course, also the case that $A_1 = L_1 - C_1$ (EQU 4).
Thus, inserting (EQU 3) in (EQU 2), we get:

$$C_0 + R_1 - E_1 = C_1$$

Inserting this in (EQU 4), we get:

$$A_1 = L_1 + C_0 + R_1 - E_1$$

Rearranging this, we get:

$$A_1 + E_1 = L_1 + C_0 + R_1$$

That is, the items on the left (assets and expenses) are all the debits, which are seen to equal the items on the right (liabilities, capital and revenues) which are all the credits. This is a basic principle of double entry.

Accounting period. See FINANCIAL YEAR (UK) and FISCAL YEAR (US).

Accounting policies. – the detailed methods of valuation and measurement which a particular company has chosen from those generally accepted by law, accounting standards or commercial practice. These policies must be used consistently, and must be disclosed (this is required in the UK, for example, by the Accounting Standard (SSAP 2) and by Company Law). A company's ANNUAL REPORT will include a 'statement of accounting policies' that have been applied in the financial statements.
Examples of disclosure of policies would include whether a company was using straight-line or reducing balance DEPRECIATION; whether it

was using FIFO or average cost for INVENTORY/stock valuation; and how it was treating provisions for future pension payments.

Accounting principles. The word 'principles' is a slight problem in accounting. In the USA it tends to mean conventions of practice, whereas in the UK it means something more fundamental and theoretical. Thus the American 'GENERALLY ACCEPTED ACCOUNTING PRINCIPLES' encompasses a wide range of broad and detailed accounting rules of practice. In the UK, the detailed rules are often called practices, policies or bases; and broader matters like ACCRUALS or CONSERVATISM were traditionally referred to as concepts or conventions.

However, perhaps because lawyers (and those in Brussels at that) were involved in the drafting of the EEC FOURTH DIRECTIVE which led to the 1981 Companies Act in the UK, British usage is now more confused. The 1981 Act referred to five broad 'principles' of accounting: GOING CONCERN, CONSISTENCY, PRUDENCE, MATCHING and individual valuation. The first four were all to be found in the UK's SSAP 2, described as 'concepts'.

The problem with these broad principles, in any country, is that there is potential for conflict. For example, in a going concern, the matching concept suggests that development costs ought to be carried forward and matched against the future revenues that they are designed to create (see RESEARCH AND DEVELOPMENT). However, prudence suggests that, because it is *possible* that no benefits will arise, all research and development costs should be immediately charged as expenses. This would also lead to greater consistency. Similar remarks would apply to advertising expenditure.

In the USA, conservatism and consistency win in the shape of SFAS 2, which does not allow the capitalization of research and development costs. In the UK, the initial exposure draft (ED 14) followed that precedent, but after complaints from heavy R and D spenders, ED 17 and the subsequent SSAP 13 allowed capitalization of development expenditure under prudent conditions.

Under SSAP 2, prudence is required to override other conventions when there is conflict. Under UK company law, no such provision exists. It is fortunate, then, that these mandatory principles are vague and may be broken in (disclosed) special circumstances or in order to allow a TRUE AND FAIR VIEW.

There are many other accounting conventions, such as MATERIALITY and MONEY MEASUREMENT.

Accounting Principles Board (APB). – set up in the USA in 1959 by the AMERICAN INSTITUTE OF CPAs (AICPA). It replaced the AICPA's Committee on Accounting Procedure, which between 1939 and 1959 had issued 51 ACCOUNTING RESEARCH BULLETINS. The APB lasted until it too was replaced, in 1973, by the FINANCIAL ACCOUNTING STANDARDS BOARD (FASB).

The APB issued 31 'Opinions' and 4 'Statements'. In many cases these have not been replaced by subsequent standards, and thus remain part of GENERALLY ACCEPTED ACCOUNTING PRINCIPLES.

The demise of the APB followed the setting up of two committees by the AICPA to investigate deficiencies in the rule-making procedures. One source of dissatisfaction was alleged dominance by large accountancy firms. The Wheat Committee reported in 1972 and led to the FASB. Another problem was seen to be the lack of a CONCEPTUAL FRAMEWORK. The Trueblood Committee's report led to the FASB's major project designed to discover or invent such a framework.

Accounting rate of return. See RATE OF RETURN.

Accounting records. See BOOKS.

Accounting reference period. See FINANCIAL YEAR.

Accounting research bulletins. – documents produced between 1939 and 1959 by the Committee on Accounting Procedure of the AMERICAN INSTITUTE OF CPAs. There were 51 such bulletins, some of which have not been superseded by the publications of the ACCOUNTING PRINCIPLES BOARD or the FINANCIAL ACCOUNTING STANDARDS BOARD.

Accounting standards. – technical accounting rules of valuation, measurement and disclosure. The exact title of accounting standards varies from country to country. The practical use of the words seems to originate officially with the Accounting Standards Steering Committee (later the ACCOUNTING STANDARDS COMMITTEE) in the UK in 1970. Standards in the UK and Ireland are called STATEMENTS OF STANDARD ACCOUNTING PRACTICE (SSAPs). In the USA, Statements of Financial Accounting Standards (SFASs) have been issued by the FINANCIAL ACCOUNTING STANDARDS BOARD since its foundation in 1973.

It is not only their titles that vary. In the UK, in 1986, the number of standards was in the twenties; in the USA in the eighties. In the UK the standards are backed by the professional bodies of accountants to which auditors of companies belong. The standards are designed to be used in the preparation of all financial statements intended to give a TRUE AND FAIR VIEW, and the latter is required by company law for all companies. Thus, the sanction for a company whose directors break standards is a qualification of the AUDIT REPORT. Also, the standards would be influential in a court of law that was determining whether a set of financial statements gave a true and fair view.

In the USA, the standards of the FASB form part of GENERALLY ACCEPTED ACCOUNTING PRINCIPLES, which are insisted upon by the SECURITIES AND EXCHANGE COMMISSION (SEC). Thus they have greater force than UK standards, but only for the relatively small proportion of companies registered with the SEC. In Canada, the professionally set standards are given legal backing.

Standards are often criticized for being inconsistent with each other and for not being based on a CONCEPTUAL FRAMEWORK. They may be criticized by practical accountants for constraining the room to manoeuvre or to give a fair view. They may be criticized by the financial press and users for still allowing too much room for arbitrary or misleading accounting practices.

A list of UK and Irish Exposure Drafts and Standards by subject follows. The US list would take up too many pages! However, the content matter is similar, and a comparison with some UK standards is shown under INTERNATIONAL ACCOUNTING STANDARDS COMMITTEE.

Several standards have been controversial. For example, in the UK there have been changes of mind on DEFERRED TAX and INVESTMENT PROPERTIES. In the USA, FOREIGN CURRENCY TRANSLATION has been a notorious problem. In all English-speaking countries, INFLATION ACCOUNTING has appeared to be an intractible problem.

In 1983, it was decided that guidelines with less force than standards could be issued in the UK, called STATEMENTS OF RECOMMENDED PRACTICE.

UK Accounting Standards and Exposure Drafts

Exposure		Date of Draft	Date and number of SSAP	Draft
ED 1	Accounting for the Results of Associated Companies	1970	January 1971	SSAP 1
ED 25	ditto	1979	SSAP amended April 1982	
ED 2	Disclosure of Accounting Policies	1971	November 1971	SSAP 2
ED 3	Accounting for Acquisitions and Mergers	1971	Replaced by ED 31	
ED 31	Accounting for Acquisitions and Mergers	1982	March 1985	SSAP 23

UK Accounting Standards and Exposure Drafts

Exposure Draft	Date of Draft	Date and number of SSAP	
ED 4 Earnings per Share	1971	February 1972 (rev Aug 74)	SSAP 3
ED 5 Extraordinary Items and Prior Year Adjustments	1971	Replaced by ED 7	–
ED 7 Accounting for Extraordinary Items	1972	April 1974	SSAP 6
ED 16 Supplement to SSAP 6	1975		
ED 36 Extraordinary Items and Prior Year Adjustments	1985	SSAP amended July 1986	
ED 6 Stocks and Work in Progress	1972	May 1975	SSAP 9
ED 8 Accounting for Changes in the Purchasing Power of Money	1973	May 1974	PSSAP 7 (provisional)
ED 18 Current Cost Accounting	1976	Replaced by ED 24	
ED 24 Current Cost Accounting	1979	March 1980	SSAP 16
ED 35 Accounting for the Effects of Changing Prices	1984		
ED 9 The Accounting Treatment of Grants	1973	April 1974	SSAP 4
ED 10 Accounting for Value Added Tax	1973	April 1974	SSAP 5
ED 11 Accounting for Deferred Taxation	1973	August 1975	SSAP 11 replaced by SSAP 15

UK Accounting Standards and Exposure Drafts

Exposure Draft	Date of Draft	Date and number of SSAP	
ED 19 Accounting for Deferred Taxation	1977	October 1978	SSAP 15
ED 33 Accounting for Deferred Tax	1983	SSAP amended May 1985	
ED 12 The Treatment of Taxation under the Imputation System in the Accounts of Companies	1973	August 1974 Appendix added December 1977	SSAP 8
ED 13 Statements of Source and Application of Funds	1974	July 1975	SSAP 10
ED 14 Accounting for Research and Development	1975	replaced by ED 17	
ED 17 Accounting for Research and Development	1976	December 1977	SSAP 13
ED 15 Accounting for Depreciation	1975	December 1977	SSAP 12
ED 26 Accounting for Investment Properties	1980	November 1981	SSAP 19
ED 37 Accounting for Depreciation	1985	SSAP amended January 1987	
ED 20 Group Accounts	1977	September 1978	SSAP 14
ED 21 Accounting for Foreign Currency Transactions	1977	replaced by ED 27	
ED 27 Accounting for Foreign Currency Translations	1980	April 1983	SSAP 20
ED 22 Accounting for Post Balance Sheet Events	1978	August 1980	SSAP 17

UK Accounting Standards and Exposure Drafts

Exposure Draft	Date of Draft	Date and number of SSAP	
ED 23 Accounting for Contingencies	1978	August 1980	SSAP 18
ED 28 Petroleum Revenue Tax	1981		
ED 29 Accounting for Leases	1981	August 1984	SSAP 21
ED 30 Accounting for Goodwill	1982	December 1984	SSAP 22
ED 32 Disclosure of Pension Information in Company Accounts	1983		
ED 34 Pension Scheme Accounts	1984	June 1986	SORP 1
ED 38 Accounting by Charities	1986		
ED 39 Accounting for Pension Costs	1986		

Accounting Standards Committee. – UK body that sets ACCOUNT-ING STANDARDS. The ASC was set up in 1970 (known until 1976, as the Accounting Standards Steering Committee) by the Institute of Chartered Accountants in England and Wales (ICAEW) soon joined by the five other major UK and Irish accountancy bodies: the Institute of Chartered Accountants of Scotland, the Institute of Chartered Accountants in Ireland, the Chartered Association of Certified Accountants, the Chartered Institute of Management Accountants and the Chartered Institute of Public Finance and Accountancy.

The cause of the setting up of the Committee was a gradual loss of confidence in the profession's technical rules. This was caused partly by several scandals and catastrophes. For example, in October 1967, during a contested takeover by GEC, Associated Electrical Industries Ltd (AEI) forecast a profit of £10m for 1967. In July 1968 a loss of £4.5m was reported instead. Accounting for the difference, the former joint auditors of AEI attributed 'roughly £5m to adverse differences which are matters substantially of fact rather than judgement and the balance of some £9.5m to adjustments which remain substantially matters of judgement'. Other disquieting events were the collapse of Rolls Razor and the bid by Leasco Data Processing Equipment Corporation for Pergamon Press Ltd.

At the end of 1969, the ICAEW published a 'Statement of Intent on Accounting Standards in the 1970s', which led to the formation of what was to become the ASC. However, controversy was not over. As a result of various criticisms, including the lack of representation of users, a review committee under the chairmanship of the ASC's chairman was set up. The 'Watts Report', *Setting Accounting Standards*, was published in 1978, and led to a change in membership and procedures of the the ASC. Instead of representatives allocated by budget contribution among the six accountancy bodies, members were to include user and government representatives.

The ASC usually approaches a new topic by issuing a consultative document for discussion. This is followed by an exposure draft, which will be the subject of comments from interested parties, and possibly a public hearing. Eventually an accounting standard will be drafted and sent to the councils of the six UK and Irish member bodies for approval. A list of standards and exposure drafts is shown under ACCOUNTING STANDARDS.

The greatest area of difficulty for the standard setters has been arriving at an acceptable, workable and effective standard on price change accounting (see INFLATION ACCOUNTING). A further, more general, problem has been the lack of a CONCEPTUAL FRAMEWORK on which to base accounting standards. Without this, discussions tend to be seen by some as too pragmatic and subject to the influence of special interest groups.

For a comparison with the USA, see FINANCIAL ACCOUNTING STANDARDS BOARD.

Accounts. – records of all the book-keeping entries relating to a particular item. For example, the wages account would record all the payments of wages. An account in the DOUBLE ENTRY system has a debit side (left) and a credit side (right). Often accounts are referred to as T-accounts, because of the rulings on the page that divide the left from the right and underline the title. A business may have thousands of accounts, including one for each debtor and creditor.

In the early days of accounting, there were only personal accounts (for people who owed and were owed money). Later, there were 'real' accounts for property of various sorts; and 'nominal' accounts for impersonal, unreal items like wages and electricity. Accounts may be collected together in groups in Ledgers or BOOKS of account.

In the UK, 'accounts' may also mean financial statements, such as BALANCE SHEETS and PROFIT AND LOSS ACCOUNTS.

Accounts payable. – US expression for CREDITORS in the UK. These are amounts owed by the business, usually as a result of purchases in the normal course of trade from suppliers who allow the business to pay at some point after purchase. Discounts will often be allowed for early payment of such accounts. The total of accounts payable at the period end form part of CURRENT LIABILITIES on a balance sheet.

Accounts receivable. – US expression for DEBTORS in the UK. These are the amounts to be paid to the business by outsiders, normally as a result of sales to customers who have not yet settled their bills. Accounts receivable are valued at the amount of the accounts, less an allowance (provision in UK terminology) for any amounts thought likely to be uncollectable. Those which are fairly certain to be uncollectable are BAD DEBTS; and there may also be allowances for specific amounts expected to be uncollectable, and general allowances against the total of accounts receivable. The general allowances would be calculated in the light of past experience with bad debts. All these allowances reflect the perceived need for CONSERVATISM, particularly in the valuation of such CURRENT ASSETS. After taking into account all these provisions, the total of accounts receivable will be part of current assets on a balance sheet.

Accruals convention. – an expression sometimes used to describe the standard practice of concentrating on the period to which an expense or revenue relates rather than on the period in which cash is paid or received. It is also known as the MATCHING principle, particularly in North America. More details are given under that heading.

Accrued expenses. – those which relate to a year but will not be paid until the following year. They result from the need regularly to draw up financial statements at a fixed time (for example, at the end of a company's year).

During a year, electricity will be used or properties will be rented, yet at the year end the related bills may not have been paid. Thus, at the year end, 'accrued' expenses are charged against income by accountants even though cash has not been paid nor perhaps the bills even received. The DOUBLE ENTRY for this is the creation of a CURRENT LIABILITY on the balance sheet. This practice may apply also to wages and salaries, taxes, and so on. An allocation of amounts to 'this year' and 'next year' may be necessary where a supplier's account straddles two accounting years. The practice is an example of the use of the MATCHING concept.

Similarly, some accounts of suppliers which are paid in any year may be wholly or partly paid on behalf of the activities of the next year. In this case, the relevant expenses for the year will have to be adjusted downwards by the accountant, and a CURRENT ASSET called 'prepayments' recorded on the balance sheet. Thus, payments of property taxes and insurance premiums may be partly prepayments.

Accumulated depreciation. – the total amount by which the accounting value of a fixed asset has so far been reduced to take account of the fact that it is wearing out or becoming obsolete (see DEPRECIATION).

Acid test. – name sometimes given to a ratio of some of a business' liquid assets to some of its short-term debts. It is thus one test of the likelihood of liquidity problems. It is also called the QUICK RATIO. For details, see that entry and CURRENT RATIO.

Acquisitions and mergers. See CONSOLIDATED FINANCIAL STATEMENTS.

Advance corporation tax (ACT). – part of the UK and Irish corporation tax systems. As its name suggests, it is an advance payment of part of the corporation tax liability of a company. The tax is triggered by the payment of a dividend, and its size is proportionate to the size of the dividend. For details, see CORPORATION TAX.

Agency theory. – an application in accounting research of theories from economics and the behavioural sciences. It is suggested that directors and other managers (the agents), particularly those of a large company, have many other aims than that of maximizing the long-run wealth of the owners of the company, the shareholders (the principals). Thus, the behaviour of managers with respect, for example, to dividend policy or the choice of accounting policies will only be predictable by assuming self-interest and studying what that would lead to.

When it comes to choosing accounting policies or to lobbying for or against particular changes in ACCOUNTING STANDARDS, managers may consider the effects of the change on declared profit figures. This may involve them in considerations of the effects on their compensation schemes or their reputations as managers if profits seem too small, and on government interference or special taxes if profits seem too large.

This problem of the inefficiencies that may result from the separation of management from ownership is also important in more general considerations of the theory of the behaviour of companies.

Aktiengesellschaft (AG). – a West German (or Swiss) public company. It literally means a 'shares' company. There are about 2,000 such companies in West Germany, which is very few compared to the number of UK PUBLIC COMPANIES. See WEST GERMANY.

Allowances. – US expression for PROVISIONS, i.e. amounts charged against profit in anticipation of reductions in value. For an example, see BAD DEBTS.

American Accounting Association (AAA). – a body whose primary membership is accounting academics in the USA. It organizes large conferences each summer, in a North American city, at which research is discussed and University recruitment carried out. It also publishes the prestigious academic journal, *The Accounting Review*. Because of the importance of university education as part of the training of members of the American profession, the AAA has had a significant impact on the development of the profession and its technical rules.

American Institute of CPAs. The American Institute of Certified Public Accountants (AICPA) was founded in 1887 (as a predecessor body). It has approximately 200,000 members. It is responsible for ethical guidance for the profession; for setting auditing standards that lead to GENERALLY ACCEPTED AUDITING STANDARDS; and for an examination system. Until 1973, it was also responsible for ACCOUNTING STANDARDS, but that role has now been taken over by the FINANCIAL ACCOUNTING STANDARDS BOARD. However, the AICPA still provides comment on the agenda and exposure drafts of standard setters.

Just as companies in the USA must be registered by state rather than federally, so CPAs must belong to a state body of CPAs. The total number of such CPAs somewhat exceeds those who have joined the AICPA. The rules for entry to the state CPA societies varies from state to state.

Amortization. – a word used, particularly in North America, to refer to certain types of DEPRECIATION, particularly that due mainly to the passing of time.

Analytical review. – one method of audit testing, which may be used as a complement to computations, verbal enquiries, inspection of records, etc. It involves the review of financial statements, accounting records and other documents for unusual items or for the reasonableness of totals.

Anglo-saxon accounting. Although financial reporting practices in the English-speaking world vary from country to country (just as the use of the language does), there is a common origin and a common philosophy behind them all. As with the predominant language, the financial reporting practices of the USA, Canada, Australia, New Zealand and Ireland are British in origin. In the case of the USA, the practices of London, Manchester, Glasgow and Edinburgh were exported in the late 19th and early 20th centuries in the most obvious of ways, that is by British accountants emigrating. For example, Arthur Young, James Marwick and Roger Mitchell (names incorporated in BIG EIGHT firms) moved from Glasgow to the USA.

Perhaps the most obvious common characteristic is the emphasis on FAIR PRESENTATION. In the USA and Canada, this is expressed as a requirement for financial statements to be fairly presented. In other countries above, the requirement is to show a 'TRUE AND FAIR VIEW'. This includes use of several ACCOUNTING PRINCIPLES mentioned under that heading, and also substantial use of the concept of MATERIALITY, whereby unimportant amounts are not shown or not necessarily treated exactly correctly. Another relevant expression here is 'substance over form', whereby figures are shown in accordance with economic reality rather than legal form.

The Netherlands also tends to have accouting of a similar type, as of course do many members of the British Commonwealth. The obvious contrast is the legal/tax basis of accounting in FRANCE or WEST GERMANY.

The differences between these two main types of accounting probably arise from the English common law system (as opposed to codified continental law), the importance of private shareholders as providers of finance (as opposed to bankers and governments), and the lack of importance of tax rules for financial reporting in the Anglo-Saxon world. Some evidence for the differences may be seen under STOCK EXCHANGES and ACCOUNTANCY PROFESSION.

Annual general meeting (AGM). – in the UK, the meeting at which shareholders may question directors on the contents of the ANNUAL REPORT and financial statements; vote on the directors' recommendation for dividends; vote on replacements for retiring members of the board; and conduct other business within the rules laid down by their company's MEMORANDUM and ARTICLES OF ASSOCIATION. The AGM of a company is held once a year; to be more exact under UK law, there must be a gap of no more than 18 months between AGMs.

The AGM is normally a quiet affair at which the Chairman gives his report for the year, listened to by a minority of the shareholders, who may then be treated to a reception. Many shareholders vote by proxy in advance. However, controversies sometimes arise over the ACCOUNTABILITY of the directors for the shareholders' resources.

Under certain conditions, Extraordinary General Meetings are also held at the request of the directors or shareholders. Normally, they are due to some crisis.

The equivalent US expression is 'annual meeting of stockholders'.

Annual report. – a document sent to shareholders after a company's year end. It contains a report by the president or chairman of the board, a review of the year or report by directors, the financial statements and notes, and the report of the auditors.

The report of the chairman (UK) or president (USA) is usually couched in fairly vague terms. It outlines the progress and problems of the year, and looks forward to the opportunities of the future. It tends to thank the staff and customers, and possibly to make a political point or two.

The DIRECTORS' REPORT (UK) or review of the year (US) contains much more detailed financial information, much of it required to be disclosed by law or accounting standards.

The annual report will also contain a summary of important figures over several years, and highlighted figures for the year.

Appreciation. – an increase in value (usually NET REALIZABLE VALUE) of an asset. Under a strict HISTORICAL COST ACCOUNTING system, such appreciation is not recognized in the accounting records of the business until the asset is sold and the gain is realized. This is the case in the USA. It is partly because of CONSERVATISM and partly because of the need for OBJECTIVITY; before the asset is sold one cannot be sure exactly what its market value is. Also, in a GOING CONCERN, the market value of fixed assets is not necessarily of interest to the users of financial statements. However, most systems of INFLATION ACCOUNTING make adjustments to asset values to record appreciation.

In the UK and several other countries, the rules about recognizing appreciation are more permissive (see REVALUATION).

A further controversy concerns the depreciation of assets which are appreciating. At first sight, it may seem incorrect to charge depreciation on an asset which is growing in value. However, depreciation is not designed to measure the value of an asset, but to represent a charge for its wearing out. Thus, if the asset is recognized as being more valuable than before, the depreciation charge for wearing it out (say by 10 per cent in a particular year) ought to become *larger* in money terms. In the UK, for example, the accounting standard, SSAP 12, confirms this. However, the Accounting Standards Committee was persuaded to issue a special standard (SSAP 19) for INVESTMENT PROPERTIES, which calls for annual revaluation and no depreciation of such properties.

In the case of inventories/stocks, appreciation is more rapidly turned into realized gains because inventories are constantly turning over. However, if the business is to maintain the same level of inventories, the gain will have to be ploughed back into replacement inventories. Thus inventory appreciation may not be a real profit but may be in danger of being taxed. Governments have responded to this problem. In the USA, businesses are allowed to use LIFO as an inventory valuation method (this usually reduces profits). In the UK, a special stock appreciation relief applied between 1973 and 1984 in the calculation of taxable profit (see STOCK RELIEF).

Similarly, systems of INFLATION ACCOUNTING tend to adjust profits downwards by a 'cost of sales adjustment' to correct for this.

See, also DEPRECIATION and ASSET VALUATION.

Appropriation account. – an expression sometimes used to describe that part below the profit and loss account or income statement where the net profit for the year is appropriated to the owners or ploughed back into the business. Appropriations are, then, ways of using up profit once it has been calculated. Dividends are appropriations, as are transfers to various RESERVES. Thus these amounts are *not* expenses of the running of the business. It is not clear whether to regard taxation as an expense or as an appropriation.

In the published financial statements of companies, appropriations are made as a continuation of the profit and loss account or income statement. In the financial statements of partnerships the appropriation account will normally be a more obvious separate account, including of course the splitting up of the profit to the various partners.

In the USA, the expression 'statement of retained earnings' is more usual.

Articles of association. – a document drawn up at the foundation of a company, setting out the rights and duties of the shareholders and directors, and the relationship between one class of shareholders and another. (See, also, MEMORANDUM.) In the USA, similar rules will be found in the BYLAWS.

Asset. – generally, something owned that has future economic benefits. However, it turns out that to define exactly what an accountant means by an 'asset' is exceptionally difficult. Various attempts have been made, particularly in the USA. A recent definition is contained in part of the CONCEPTUAL FRAMEWORK project in the USA (in Statement of Financial Accounting Concepts, 3). According to that document, the existence of an asset relies upon 'probable future economic benefits obtained or controlled by a particular entity as a result of past transactions or events'.

Using that definition (or, indeed, common sense) many items are obviously assets, like the inventories/stocks, cash balances, machines and buildings owned by a company. The problems arise in more marginal cases (see below). Those items that are recognized by accountants as assets can be divided into FIXED ASSETS and CURRENT ASSETS. Some assets are tangible, like machines and cash; others are INTANGIBLE like goodwill.

When all the assets in the balance sheet are added together, the result will be the 'total assets'. When the amounts due to outsiders (the

LIABILITIES) are deducted, what remains is the NET ASSETS or net worth of the business. Of course, because of the unrecorded assets and the sometimes curious valuation conventions of accountants, the 'net worth' is probably much less than the business is worth! (See below and, also, ASSET VALUATION.)

There are several problems with the definition of assets. For example, are machines which are on long LEASES to be considered as assets of the lessee? Legally they still belong to the lessor, but in many cases the economic substance of the initial leasing transaction is very similar to a purchase plus a loan. In recent years, the practice in the USA and the UK has moved towards treating many leased assets as those of the lessee.

A second example is a new highway. It may be of great benefit to a company, and some of the company's taxes may have helped to pay for it. Also the company has rights to its use. However, the highway does not belong to the company, and is fairly clearly not the company's asset. Equally straightforwardly, substantial expense may be involved in the drilling of an oil well, only to discover that it is a 'dry hole'. Since it will bring no future benefits, it is not counted as an asset (but, see OIL AND GAS ACCOUNTING).

In the case of some companies, like Marks and Spencer in the UK or McDonald's Hamburgers, the most important 'assets' do not appear at all on the balance sheet. The value of such companies rests on their future earning power which rests upon customer loyalty, brand names, trained staff, skilled management and so on. These items are generally not treated as assets by accountants because their valuation would not be OBJECTIVE. It is not at all clear exactly what they are worth or exactly what has been spent to create them. Yet, they are owned, they will bring future benefit, and amounts are constantly expended to create or preserve them. However, when a business is sold, an amount in excess of the accounting value of the assets may be paid. In the financial statements of the purchaser, this excess may be recorded as an asset called GOODWILL.

Thus, the accounting definition of an asset is heavily hemmed in by a number of conventions, all of which have good reasons behind them. However, the net result is not necessarily easily comprehensible or satisfactory.

Asset-stripping. Asset-stripping or financial surgery was particularly popular in the late 1960s and early 1970s. It is normally associated with the purchase of a business by financial entrepreneurs who have calculated that the asking price for the business as a going concern is lower than the total amount that could be raised by selling the assets separately. Normally it is land and buildings which may be particularly valuable. The HISTORICAL COST ACCOUNTING convention may lead to such assets being recorded at a small fraction of their NET REALIZABLE VALUE. Owners of a business who are not very good at interpreting financial statements may be misled into parting with their business at an unreasonably low price. The assets in their existing use may be not very profitable, but they may be able to be sold at a high price. In this sense, perhaps the asset-stripper is not only doing himself a service, for the assets will pass from a poor use to a more valuable one.

In order to ensure that the government also gains from this activity, various taxes have been introduced, such as those on capital gains.

Asset valuation. The traditional method of valuation in accounting is HISTORICAL COST ACCOUNTING, whereby assets are valued at purchase price or production cost, less DEPRECIATION (i.e. at net historical cost). There are good reasons for this, such as CONSERVATISM and a desire for OBJECTIVITY. However, particularly when prices have risen, the historical cost of an asset may be misleading, given that many non-accountants assume that assets are recorded at a market price. In some countries, including the UK but not the USA, land and buildings are sometimes revalued to reflect the increase in what they could be sold for. The problem is that there are few rules: some companies revalue annually, some every five years, some never.

FIXED ASSETS other than land and buildings tend to be more uniformly shown at net historical cost, though it should be remembered that depreciation is not an exact measurement.

CURRENT ASSETS are valued at the lower of cost and net realizable value, though in North America replacement cost is sometimes used where it is even lower. DEBTORS/ACCOUNTS RECEIVABLE are valued at what one prudently expects to receive, and CASH is valued at its face value.

Under systems of INFLATION ACCOUNTING, asset values will be increased (or decreased) to NET REALIZABLE VALUE or net CURRENT REPLACEMENT COST or ECONOMIC VALUE, or they may be inflation indexed.

In the Netherlands, some companies use net current replacement cost as their main valuation system. In France, all companies were required to revalue, using government indices, as at 31 December 1976; subsequent purchases are valued at historical cost.

Thus, asset valuation varies dramatically from country to country and even within a country. It is important to understand the rules of the relevant country when attempting to interpret a balance sheet; and then to read the notes attached to a company's financial statement. Perhaps, above all, it should be understood that conventional accounting does not really intend to present a 'valuation' at all, but a figure that results from the rules of accounting.

Associated companies. – a British term for a company over which another has significant influence. The term is not so well known in the USA. In both countries, the 'Equity Method' is used for such companies. A company will be presumed to be an associated company if it is owned to the extent of 20 per cent to 50 per cent. Above 50 per cent ownership it becomes a subsidiary; under 20 per cent ownership it becomes a trade investment (see CONSOLIDATED FINANCIAL STATEMENTS). Companies held as joint ventures with other owners will be treated as associated companies.

The term is spreading to other English-speaking countries, in many of which the Equity Method, as described below, is also used. The rules in the USA may be found in APB Opinion 18 and SFAS 35. In the UK, the relevant rules are in SSAP 1 (as amended). Partly as a result of the seventh DIRECTIVE OF THE EEC, the Anglo-Saxon practice will be spreading further.

The appropriate treatment for such a partly-owned company in the CONSOLIDATED FINANCIAL STATEMENTS of the owner is to record it in the balance sheet as a single line, perhaps called 'Investment in Associated Company'. It is valued at the cost of the investment in the company at the time of purchase *plus* the appropriate proportion of the undistributed profits made by the associated company since that date (in the UK, the cost will be split into the appropriate proportion of the fair value of the assets and the implied goodwill).

Dividends passing from the associated company to its owner cause cash to increase and 'investment in associated company' to decrease by the same amount. Profits earned by the associated compny cause the owner's consolidated profits to be increased by the appropriate share, and 'investment in associated company' to rise by the same amount.

In France an alternative method of treating joint ventures is practised, called PROPORTIONAL CONSOLIDATION.

Auditing. The basic aim of a modern audit in the UK or the USA is to give an opinion on whether the financial statements drawn up by the directors of a company give a FAIR PRESENTATION (USA) or a TRUE AND FAIR VIEW (UK). In order to do this an auditor needs to check the physical existence and valuation of important assets; and he needs to examine the systems of INTERNAL CONTROL to ensure that transactions are likely to have been recorded correctly. If internal control is poor he will ask for it to be improved and he will increase the amount of checking done on sample transactions. If the control systems look good, relatively small samples of various types of transactions may be checked.

The auditor would generally be expected to circularize a sample of some of the debtors to confirm that they exist. He would normally attend the count of the inventory (in the UK, the annual stock take). He would try to spot and to question unusual items in the books of account or financial statements. The rules for auditing vary from firm to firm, but are to some extent found in AUDITING STANDARDS.

The directors and auditors will be hoping that the AUDIT REPORT can be 'unqualified', as a result of the relevant laws and standards being followed, and the overall impression of a fair view being given. In order to achieve this, the auditors will try to persuade the directors to make any necessary changes to the published accounts.

Auditing is a very ancient activity. By derivation, it means 'hearing' (*audit* is Latin for 'he hears'). Auditing was thus originally the process whereby the owner heard the account given by his steward of the use of the owner's resources for a period (see STEWARDSHIP). By the nineteenth century, the many owners of a large company would appoint one of their number to be a specific auditor of the financial statement prepared by the directors whom they had appointed to manage the company. This was partly because the process of auditing had become more complicated as business itself became more complicated.

In the UK, audit became compulsory for limited liability banks as a result of the 1879 Companies Act which followed the spectacular failure of the City of Glasgow Bank in 1878. The 1900 Companies Act made audit compulsory for all companies. In the USA, audit is compulsory for companies registered with the SECURITIES AND EXCHANGE COMMISSION.

'Oh Lord! It's the auditors!'

The qualifications that auditors must have are also set down: membership of a CPA body in the USA, or in the UK membership of one of four of the bodies of the CONSULTATIVE COMMITTEE OF THE ACCOUNTANCY BODIES (or some other individuals recognized by the relevant government department). This provides a large amount of government-required work for accountants of recognized institutes. It is the single most important type of work for the members of these bodies, although many members do work in other fields. Auditing is now very complex, so high standards of training are necessary. Entry standards and examinations are now of high quality.

In Anglo-Saxon countries, auditing is carried out by individuls or by firms which vary greatly in size. Some firms have hundreds of partners and thousands of staff. However, the audit is always the ultimate responsibility of a member of one of the appropriate professional bodies.

Also see INTERNAL AUDIT.

Auditing Practices Committee. – the committee of the CONSULTA-TIVE COMMITTEE OF THE ACCOUNTANCY BODIES that is responsible for preparing AUDITING STANDARDS and Guidelines in the UK. The standards have the backing of the professional bodies of accountants. The first 'standard' was issued in 1980. The standards include: 'The Auditors' Operational Standard', 'The Audit Report' and 'Qualifications in Audit Reports'.

Audit report. – the report of independent auditors that is required on all annual financial statements of companies in the UK, and all those registered with the SECURITIES AND EXCHANGE COMMISSION in the USA.

In the English-speaking world the audit report tends to be relatively short. Examples are shown below:

> (US) In our opinion, the consolidated financial statements appearing on pages 25 through 36 present fairly the financial position of the Corporation and its subsidiary companies at December 31, 198X and 198X, and the results of their operations and the changes in their financial position for each of the three years in the period ended December 31, 198X, in conformity with generally accepted accounting principles consistently applied. Our examinations of these statements were made in accordance with generally accepted auditing standards and accordingly included such tests of the accounting records and such other auditing procedures as we considered necessary in the circumstances.

> (UK) We have audited the accounts on pages 5 and 13 to 21, in accordance with approved auditing standards. In our

opinion the accounts, which have been prepared under the historical cost convention, modified to include the revaluation of certain properties, give a true and fair view of the state of affairs of the Company and the Group at March 31 198X and of the profit and source and application of funds of the Group, for the 52 weeks then ended, and comply with the Companies Acts.

In the USA, reference is made in audit reports to FAIR PRESENTATION, GENERALLY ACCEPTED ACCOUNTING PRINCIPLES, consistency of application and GENERALLY ACCEPTED AUDITING STANDARDS. In the UK, reference is made to Company Law and to 'a true and fair view'; compliance with ACCOUNTING STANDARDS is implied unless there is a statement to the contrary.

The auditors are required by the professional body of accountants to which they belong to disclose breaches of the rules mentioned above. In some other countries, notably in continental Europe, there is a long-form report which is written by auditors to shareholders and management. It tells of more general breaches of the law and perceived dangers to the company.

Also, auditors in the Anglo-Saxon world may send a 'management letter', to the management of the company only, outlining deficiencies in INTERNAL CONTROL systems or other areas where improvements would be useful.

Auditing standards. – rules for the practice of auditors, formalized more recently than the technical rules of ACCOUNTING STANDARDS. The rules contain ethical guidelines as well as detailing the work to be covered by an audit and the standard practice for the AUDIT REPORT. The rules have been drawn up by committees of the ACCOUNTANCY PROFESSION, for example the AUDITING PRACTICES COMMITTEE in the UK (see that entry for some examples of UK standards). In the USA, the standards taken together become GENERALLY ACCEPTED AUDITING STANDARDS (GAAS).

Australia. Australian accounting practice may reasonably be included as part of ANGLO-SAXON ACCOUNTING, with its emphasis on FAIR PRESENTATION and reporting on shareholders. Clearly, the original source of accounting and many of the accountancy firms was Britain. Practice is broadly similar to that in the UK.

The professional bodies are the Institute of Chartered Accountants in Australia and the Australian Society of Accountants. The membership of the former is more concentrated in the auditing profession. Some facts about these bodies are under ACCOUNTANCY PROFESSION. Membership of these bodies, like those in the USA and Scotland, for example, is drawn from among those with RELEVANT DEGREES.

ACCOUNTING STANDARDS in Australia are overseen by the government-backed Australian Accounting Standards Review Board.

Authorized share capital. – the maximum amount of a particular type of share in a particular company that may be issued. The amount is laid down in the company's MEMORANDUM (UK) or CERTIFICATE OF INCORPORATION (US). It may be interesting information to shareholders as it puts a limit on the number of co-owners. The memorandum can be varied by a sufficient majority of the shareholders. See also ORDINARY SHARES and PREFERENCE SHARES.

Average cost (AVCO). – in the context of INVENTORY (stocks) valuation, a method of determining the historical cost of a particular type of inventory. As its name suggests, the cost of any unit of inventory or material used is deemed to be the average of the unit costs at which the inventory was bought. The average can be worked out at set intervals or each time there is a further purchase. AVCO is a minority practice in the UK and the USA. See FIFO and LIFO.

B

Backlog depreciation. If a company bases DEPRECIATION on current values, backlog depreciation is the amount of extra depreciation that would be necessary in a particular year in order to make up for the fact that previous years' depreciation provisions had been based on values that are now out-of-date. Most systems of INFLATION ACCOUNTING would increase ACCUMULATED DEPRECIATION for this reason but would not charge the backlog against the current year's profit, because the amount relates to previous years.

Bad debts. – amounts of DEBTORS (UK)/ACCOUNTS RECEIVABLE (US) that have become or are expected to become uncollectable. However, there are various levels of doubt that one may have. Normally, one would hope and expect that a great majority of debts would eventually be received. However, CONSERVATISM requires that all reasonably likely losses be anticipated. Thus, debts which are almost certainly uncollectable are deducted from the total; debts which are reasonably likely to be uncollectable have a specific provision (UK) or allowance (US) made against them; and in addition a general provision or allowance is made against the total remaining figure of debts, based on previous experience with unexpected bad debts.

In each of the three above cases, there will be an expense charged against income, and a reduction in the figure of Debtors/Accounts Receivable shown on the balance sheet.

Balance sheet. – a snap-shot of the accounting records of assets, liabilities and capital of a business at a particular moment, most obviously the accounting year end. The balance sheet is the longest established of the main financial statements produced by a business. As its name suggests, it is a sheet of the balances from the DOUBLE ENTRY system at a particular time. It is important to note that it is probably not a snap-shot of what the business is *worth*. This is because not all the business' items of value are recognized by accountants as ASSETS, and because the ASSET VALUATION methods used are normally based on past costs rather than on present market values.

Initially, the balance sheet was not designed as a statement of worth at all; it was merely a mechanical by-product of the periodical closing of books in the double-entry system. (In some sense, the balance sheet is the graveyard of the double-entry system; it balances because the double-entry system creates equal totals of debits and credits.) The worth of a business was more sensibly calculated by taking a quite separate 'inventory' of all the assets and liabilities at a date.

Annual balance sheets are compulsory requirements of COMPANY LAW (UK) and the SECURITIES AND EXCHANGE COMMISSION (US). Throughout most of the ANGLO-SAXON ACCOUNTING world there are no standard formats prescribed for balance sheets. However, as a result of the implementation by the 1981 Companies Act in the UK of the EEC's fourth DIRECTIVE on company law, compulsory formats for financial statements have been introduced, as discussed below.

Before the 1981 Companies Act in the UK (and still in other English-speaking countries) formats and terminology varied substantially. In the USA, many balance sheets use an 'account format' with assets on the left and capital and liabilities on the right. The CURRENT ASSETS are shown above the FIXED ASSETS (see Figure 1 below). However, some US balance sheets are shown in statement form (see Figure 2 below for a UK version). Even the title of the balance sheet may be expressed instead as 'statement of financial position' or some variation. (The numbers in the two figures are slightly different.)

In the UK, account form balance sheets were the norm until the second half of the twentieth century, and are still found for partnerships and sole traders. However, unlike US and continental European balance sheets, the assets were on the *right* and the capital and liabilities on the *left*.

However, long before the 1981 Companies Act, large companies in the UK had taken to using a statement (or vertical) format, as in Figure 2. This is because it enables the presentation of NET CURRENT ASSETS (or working capital), and because it avoids the confusion that undistributed profit might appear to be a liability. UK company law

Figure 1 *A US Account Form Balance Sheet*

JCN Inc
Balance Sheet, December 31, 198X ($000)

Current Assets			Current Liabilities		
Cash		300	Loans Payable		800
Accounts receivable		1850	Accounts Payable		1200
Inventories		1500	Accrued Expenses		400
Total		3650	Dividends		600
			Total		3000
Investments		800	Deferred Taxes		500
Properties			Long-term Debt		3000
Land	2000		Shareholders' Equity		
Buildings	2000		Common Stock	1500	
Machinery	3000		Paid-in Capital	500	
			Retained Earnings	2950	
Total		7000	Total		4950
Total Assets		11450	Total Liabs and Equity		11450

Figure 2 *A UK Statement Form*

D & D Pirana plc
Balance Sheet 31.12.198X (£000)

Fixed Assets			
Tangible Assets			
Land and Buildings			4000
Plant and Machinery			2000
Fixtures and Fittings			1000
			7000
Investments			800
			7800
Current Assets			
Stocks	1500		
Debtors	1850		
Cash at Bank and in Hand	300		
		3650	
Creditors: falling due within one year			
Bank Loans and Overdrafts	800		
Trade Creditors	1200		
Corporation Tax	800		
Proposed Dividends	600		
Accruals	100		
		3500	
Net Current Assets			150
Total Assets less Current Liabilities			7950
Creditors: falling due after one year			
Debenture Loans			3000
Capital and Reserves			
Called-up Share Capital	1500		
Share Premium	500		
Profit and Loss Account	2950		
Shareholders' Interest			4950
Long-term Liabilities and Capital			7950

(now the 1985 Companies Act) sets out two balance sheet formats and allows companies to choose (consistently) between them. One format is shown as Figure 2. The other format has very similar headings but is in account form, with the assets on the left, starting with fixed assets. The headings (as in Figure 2) must be shown in the order laid down. There is a further level of sub-headings which must either be shown on the balance sheet or, where clearer, in the notes to the balance sheet. The notes will also include other compulsory disclosures connected with balance sheet items, like cumulative amounts of DEPRECIATION. (See, also, entries for NOTES, CAPITAL COMMITMENTS and CONTINGENT LIABILITIES.)

Bankruptcy. A person is insolvent if he is unable to pay his debts as they fall due. A creditor may 'sue for bankruptcy' in order that a court may declare the person legally bankrupt which will affect his ability to undertake commercial transactions. (See, also, INSOLVENCY.)

Bear. – an investor on a STOCK EXCHANGE who anticipates falls in prices. A 'bear market' is a pessimistic state of affairs at a stock exchange. The opposite is a BULL, who charges ahead, anticipating price rises (see, also, STAG). Successful bears are those who agree to 'sell' shares that they do not yet own, in order to cover the sale by buying later when the price has fallen. On the London Stock Exchange, the gaps between ACCOUNT DAYS leave plenty of scope for this.

Below the line. The 'line' in question is that showing the 'NET PROFIT after tax' in a profit and loss account (UK) or the 'NET INCOME' in an INCOME STATEMENT (US). See ABOVE THE LINE.

Beta. The 'beta co-efficient' of a share is an indication of one aspect of the risk attached to it. The beta shows the sensitivity of the price of a share to changes in the price of shares generally. See CAPITAL ASSET PRICING MODEL.

Big Eight. – an expression used to describe the largest Anglo-American accounting firms, which have branches virtually throughout the world.

> *The Big Eight* (in alphabetical order)
> Arthur Andersen
> Arthur Young
> Coopers & Lybrand
> Deloitte, Haskins & Sells
> Ernst & Whinney
> Klynveld, Peat, Marwick, Goerdeler
> Price Waterhouse
> Touche Ross

The largest firm is Klynveld, Peat, Marwick, Goerdeler, which was formed by a merger announced in 1986. Exactly which order the firms ought to be in depends on whether you count the number of offices, number of partners, number of staff, total fee income, etc. It also depends on which year, what the exchange rates are, and whether it is for the world, the UK, the USA or some other context.

These firms are very well established throughout the Anglo-Saxon world, and increasingly in Europe. In some countries, there is resistance to their success, and firms have to operate under local names or have local partners, or they have to work through similar, legally separate, national firms.

Because of the professional requirements of accountancy bodies in the Anglo-Saxon world, these firms are organized as partnerships not as companies. Some are world-wide partnerships, others are federations of national partnerships. However they are organized, they are very large and powerful bodies, helping to spread ANGLO-SAXON ACCOUNTING throughout the world.

Most of the firms began in the UK and in the USA, and later merged. The exception is Arthur Andersen which has spread from the USA. In many cases the founders of the US parts of these multinational firms were expatriate Britons. The role of such firms outside the UK and the USA was originally to audit subsidiaries of UK or US multinationals. However, in many countries their work has now expanded to include much domestic auditing and consultancy.

Bills of exchange. – an acknowledgement of debt, for example as a result of a non-cash trading transaction. A company may of course have 'bills payable' or 'bills receivable'. Bills can be passed from one person to another, i.e. they are negotiable. Banks may be willing to 'discount' a bill, that is to give cash in exchange for the bill at a discount on its face value. See, also, DEBTORS (UK) and ACCOUNTS RECEIVABLE (US).

Bonds. – a word used to cover many sorts of (usually) long-term loans to a company or other body. For details, see DEBENTURES. The expressions 'loan stock' or, in the USA, 'obligations' or 'debt' are also used. Bonds usually have a fixed life, a fixed interest return and a fixed redemption value.

Bonus shares. – shares issued to existing shareholders of a company, in proportion to their shareholdings. They are free, as their name suggests; no cash changes hands. The purpose is usually to lower the share price, perhaps for the psychological reason that it seems high in relation to other shares or has gone into two digits of pounds (i.e. £10 or above). If a one-for-one issue is made, the result would be a doubling of shares. Since nothing else about the company has changed, the share price ought to halve; but sometimes it falls less far, perhaps because of favourable attention drawn to the company.

Accounting for the issue is straightforward; reserves of various kinds can be relabelled 'share capital' to the total value of the PAR VALUE of the shares.

Bonus issues are sometimes called 'scrip issues' or 'capitalization issues' (because reserves are being capitalized). In the USA, the equivalent expressions are STOCK DIVIDEND/SPLIT.

Bookkeeping. – day-to-day recording of transactions of a business or other body. See DOUBLE ENTRY for a detailed description. Bookkeeping describes the more mechanical everyday aspects of accounting.

Books. – the detailed records of all the transactions of a business, kept on a daily basis. They include the ACCOUNTS. Some types of transactions are so numerous that the DOUBLE ENTRY system would be swamped if they were recorded individually; for example, credit sales, credit purchases and cash transactions. For these, special subsidiary books are used to record all the details and then pass summary totals through to the main system. Thus, there may be a 'sales day book', a 'purchases day book' and a 'cash book'.

The accounting records are sometimes divided up into 'ledgers' of similar types. For example, there may be a Sales Ledger and a Purchases Ledger in which totals from the day books are 'posted'. Traditionally, there would have been personal ledgers (for amounts owed to or by persons), real ledgers (for land, buildings, etc), and nominal ledgers (for those things that were neither personal nor physical, like interest charges, depreciation and so on). However, the expression 'nominal ledger' has come to be used by some to describe all the main accounts. These days, accounting records in many businesses are kept on computer tapes, so that physical 'books' and 'ledgers' are beginning to go the way of quill pens.

UK company law requires proper accounting records to be kept, and this includes that they should be in double entry. Similar practice exists in all developed countries; because auditors need to examine such records later, and because they must be capable of inspection for legal and tax purposes.

Book value. The 'value' of the assets and liabilities of a business, as held in its ACCOUNTS. See NET BOOK VALUE.

Budget. – a financial plan, usually expressed in money terms and divided into time periods. For example, a business may have a cash budget for the coming year, detailing the planned inflows and outflows of cash on a monthly basis. This will involve the calculation of the planned surplus cash at the end of each month. There will also be sales, production, purchases, expense and other budgets.

A system of 'budgetary control' has budgets at its heart but comprises several other elements. It may be seen as part of MANAGEMENT

ACCOUNTING. The process will commence well before the beginning of the year to be budgeted for. The first step is to decide upon which factors will determine the activities of the business for the year. Normally one would start with a forecast of sales, broken down by product and time of sale (let us suppose that the whole system is organized on a monthly basis). The forecast will have to be adjusted if it is found that there are constraints on the supply of suitable raw materials for production, skilled labour or factory capacity. Forecasts of production and raw material usage will have been made in order to assist this.

Then a sales budget may be set, which is a *plan* rather than a forecast. The budget should be broken down into areas for which individual managers are responsible. For best results, the managers should have been involved in the preparation of the forecasts and budgets. It is they who have to achieve the budget and who will be held responsible for failures. Other budgets are then built up around the sales budget so that goods are available when they are designed to be sold, and so on.

The resulting cash forecasts may show deficits or substantial surpluses at particular times of the year. Deficits of cash might be disastrous, and substantial surpluses would be an inefficient use of resources. Thus, adjustments (loans, share issues, overdraft facilities, etc) will be planned before the figures become the cash *budget*. When every area of the business has been budgeted for, it will be possible to produce budgeted capital requirements and a budgeted profit and loss account or income statement. The work may be co-ordinated by a 'budget committee', and computer models may be used.

The next stage in the process begins once the business enters the period budgeted for. The accountants will provide 'actual' information for the same month and using the same headings as the budgets. Comparisons can be made, and 'variances' highlighted. The variances between 'actual' and 'budget' will be split in some cases between those caused by volume differences and those caused by price differences. Managers can then focus attention on trying to correct for these unexpected problems. Obviously, the more detailed and accurate the figures and the faster they are produced, the more likely it is that corrective action will be possible.

Because variances in one budget (like sales or production) may cause automatic variances in another (like raw materials or cash), it is sensible to use 'flexible budgeting' which can make consequent adjustments for other budgets and later months. Otherwise, the managers of raw materials or cash may be blamed for, or take action to 'correct', errors beyond their control.

A good budgeting system is probably essential for an efficient business, particularly a large one. It should improve co-ordination, crisis-avoidance, motivation, assessment of managers, prediction of profits and reaction to unexpected events.

Balls, crystal, three-year budgets for the use of . . .'

Bull. – an investor on a STOCK EXCHANGE who anticipates a rise in prices. Thus, a 'bull market' is an optimistic state of affairs at a stock exchange. Successful bulls are those who 'buy' shares, intending to sell them soon afterwards when prices have risen. Because of the gaps between ACCOUNT DAYS on the London Stock Exchange, the buying and selling may be *settled* on the same day. Thus, 'buying' can be achieved without the apparently necessary resources.

The opposite of a bull is a BEAR. Also see STAG.

Business combinations. – a US expression for acquisitions or mergers involving two or more companies. The accounting treatments can be varied and complex; see CONSOLIDATED FINANCIAL STATEMENTS.

Buy-out. – purchase of a company by a group of people containing some of the former managers of it; see MANAGEMENT BUY-OUT.

Bylaws. – the rules of a US corporation concerning the relationships between and among the board of directors and the different classes of shareholders. The bylaws need to be established, with the CERTIFICATE OF INCORPORATION, before a corporation can be properly born. In the UK the equivalent documents are the ARTICLES OF ASSOCIATION and the MEMORANDUM.

C

Called-up share capital. Newly issued shares are sometimes paid for in several instalments or calls. The called-up capital is the total amount of instalments so far due from all shareholders.

Canada. Canadian accounting, like much else in that country, has been heavily influenced by the UK and the USA. It is part of ANGLO-SAXON ACCOUNTING, including the emphasis on FAIR PRESENTATION and provision of information for shareholders. As in the UK, there is statutory legislation concerning companies and their accounting. There are also recommendations (like ACCOUNTING STANDARDS) set by the Accounting Research Committee of the Canadian Institute of Chartered Accountants (whose earliest predecessor body was founded in 1880). An important difference from the UK is that these standards are given legal backing by company law. On points of detail Canada tends to move in line with the USA rather than with the UK (e.g. DEFERRED TAX, and strict HISTORICAL COST ACCOUNTING).

Capital. – a word used somewhat loosely in the business world in general, and even by accountants. It may mean the total of a company's finance, including all share capital, past profits, long-term loans and current liabilities. This would be the total of the right-hand side of a company balance sheet (or, possibly, the left hand side for UK unincorporated businesses and businesses in many Commonwealth countries; see BALANCE SHEET). Such an aggregation might be called 'total capital'. It would, of course, equal 'total assets'.

However, 'capital' might also be used to mean the long-term finance, that is the above aggregate less current liabilities. Yet another meaning might be all the elements of capital belonging to shareholders (SHAREHOLDERS' EQUITY); or even just the amount of money contributed in the past by the shareholders. Unfortunately, the reader will have to determine the exact meaning by the context. At least you have been warned!

The expression 'capital employed' is also seen on balance sheets and in profitability RATIOS. It tends to mean the total long-term capital, although such an aggregate might be called 'net capital employed' because it does not include current liabilities.

Capital allowances. – a system of DEPRECIATION used in the determination of taxable income that is unique to the British Isles. The rates are specified in annual Finance Acts; they tend to be more generous than the depreciation that accountants would charge for financial accounting purposes. There are two main reasons for the existence of capital allowances. First, the subjective nature of depreciation is removed from the tax system. Accountants can charge the most appropriate depreciation in their accounts, without being worried that it will affect taxation. This may be a problem in some other countries. In a sense, the reverse problem occurs in most continental countries, in that tax-based depreciation rates determine accounting depreciation (see FRANCE and WEST GERMANY). The second reason is that some capital allowances are designed to act as investment incentives for the types of assets to which they apply. This ACCELERATED DEPRECIATION for tax purposes lowers the tax bill quickly and thus is a cash incentive. A somewhat similar provision exists in the USA as the INVESTMENT TAX CREDIT. In the UK, there are also examples of regional tax incentives.

From 1970 to early 1984 in the UK, the 'first year allowance' for plant and machinery was a full 100 per cent of the cost in the year of purchase. There was also a 75 per cent allowance on industrial buildings like factories. However, this system was gradually replaced; so that from 1 April 1986 there will be a uniform 25 per cent annual WRITING DOWN ALLOWANCE for plant, cars, patents and 'know how'. The allowance works on a REDUCING BALANCE basis. For industrial buildings, there is a 4 per cent allowance on a straight-line basis.

However, there are no allowances for commercial buildings, like shops or offices; and none for land, which generally does not wear out. Consequently, profitable companies in commerce rather than industry may have small capital allowances. Many of them have recently taken to buying unnecessary machinery and then leasing it to manufacturing companies (see LEASES). The commercial company claims the capital allowances and the manufacturing company, which may have reduced its taxable income to zero with its other allowances, makes lease payments.

When assets are sold, capital allowances are, in effect, reclaimed by the Inland Revenue to the extent that the sale price exceeds the tax written down value, which will usually be zero for plant and machinery.

'Unfortunately, it doesn't fall within the definition of plant for tax purposes'

Capital asset pricing model. – a theory, which may be expressed by equations, about the determination of the price of marketable securities, like shares in listed companies. The model is built up on a number of assumptions, some of which are not very realistic. It is designed to show, for a particular security, the relationship between its expected return and its risk. The total risk attached to a security can be broken down into that which is systematic (related to the rest of the securities market) and that which is unsystematic (related only to the particular security). Systematic risk cannot be avoided by diversification, but unsystematic risk can be.

In algebraic terms, the following equation is descriptive of the CAPM:

$$E(R_j) = R_f + B_j (ER_M - R_f)$$

where $E(R_j)$ is the expected return on security j; R_f is the risk-free rate of return; B_j represents systematic risk (the beta coefficient); and ER_M is the expected return on the market portfolio.

Capital commitments. – future commitments that will entail material amounts of expenditure. For example, a company may have contracted to purchase, at a future date, a new office building. At the balance sheet date, it may have no asset and no liability or cash expended as a result of the commitment. However, the commitment may be of interest to users of financial statements, particularly those concerned with the liquidity of the company. Thus, capital commitments are recorded in the Notes to the balance sheet.

Capital employed. – the aggregate finance used by a business. Sometimes the expression is used to refer to the total of all liabilities and capital; sometimes it means 'net capital employed', that is it excludes current liabilities (see CAPITAL).

Capital gains tax. – a tax on the increase in value of certain assets when realized. In the UK such a tax has operated on most assets since 1965, and has been indexed for inflation since 1982.

Capitalization. – the aggregate market price on a Stock Exchange of all the listed shares of a company, or perhaps all its ORDINARY SHARES or COMMON STOCK. It is, in a sense, what the company is worth, which may considerably exceed the balance sheet NET ASSETS. This is because balance sheets do not include all valuable assets (for example, customer loyalty or trained staff; see ASSET), and because accounting ASSET VALUATION is often not based on market prices.

Furthermore, if you tried to buy all or most of the shares in a listed company, the price would gradually rise as the total demand for them would have increased and as people would realize that someone was buying heavily. Similarly, if you owned a large block of shares (or all of them), you probably could not sell them at the amount suggested by the 'market capitalization' because the price would start falling as soon as you started selling heavily. Thus, the 'market capitalization' is a somewhat nebulous concept.

In addition, when one hears, as part of a financial report, that many millions have been wiped off the value of shares, most shareholders will not have really suffered yet, because the price of their shares only really matters at the point of purchase or sale.

Capitalization issue. – an issue of shares which turns some of a company's reserves into share capital. Existing shareholders are given the new shares free; but the share price will fall commensurately. The purpose of the exercise will probably be to cause the unit price of the shares to fall to a more psychologically appealing level for trading.

Such issues are also known as scrip issues, BONUS ISSUES or, in the USA, STOCK DIVIDENDS (see those entries for more details).

Capital maintenance. – a concept used to determine the definition of profit. It is variation in this that underlies the differences in systems of INFLATION ACCOUNTING.

Under HISTORICAL COST ACCOUNTING, the profit of a period is recognized as any excess of the money capital at the end of the period over the money capital at the beginning of the period (after correcting for additions or reductions of capital, like share issues or dividends). However, it might well be argued that there is no *real* profit unless the shareholders' capital is maintained in *real* terms, that is after adjustment to take into account the fall in value of money due to inflation. An accounting system based on this concept of capital maintenance would be called GENERAL PURCHASING POWER ACCOUNTING (GPP), or Current Purchasing Power (CPP) in the UK, or Constant Dollar Accounting or General Price Level Adjusted (GPLA) in the USA. Such systems use retail price indices to adjust accounting figures from historical cost. This is a relatively simple set of adjustments, which does take *inflation* into account. It was the method favoured by the accountancy professional bodies in the English-speaking world in the late 1960s and early 1970s. In several highly inflationary economies, such as some in South America, GPP systems have been adopted.

An alternative view of the maintenance of capital is to concentrate not on the shareholders' money capital (historical cost) nor on the shareholders' real capital (GPP), but on the physical capital of the business. This would be an ENTITY VIEW rather than a PROPRIETARY VIEW. This point of view is taken on the grounds that the business is a GOING

CONCERN and does not intend to return capital to the shareholders. Thus, for the decisions of managers and investors, the present worth, past progress and future prospects of a business can best be indicated by measuring current values and then calculating the resultant profit implications. A version of such a system, called CURRENT COST ACCOUNTING (CCA) was introduced as a requirement for supplementary financial statements of large and listed companies in the UK in 1980 (until 1985), although its exact capital maintenance concept is not crystal clear. Other English-speaking countries have adopted similar requirements. In the USA, the SEC requires disclosure of some replacement cost information. In the Netherlands, some companies have been publishing replacement cost based financial statements for decades.

Thus, how exactly one measures profit depends upon which concept of capital one has adopted.

Capital redemption reserve. – an amount of profit set aside as undistributable when shares are bought back by a UK company. This is unusual, because it is a long-established principle of law and accounting that, in order to protect CREDITORS, the share capital of a company should not be paid back to the owners unless the company is wound up, in which case the creditors would be ahead of the shareholders in the legal order of payment. Similarly, there are rules about the determination of DISTRIBUTABLE PROFITS, to ensure that shareholders can only receive dividends in respect of REALIZED profits. Thus, it was a requirement of UK company law, and that of other commonwealth countries, that ordinary shares were not redeemable. However, as part of the UK's 1981 Companies Act (now the 1985 Act), the possibility of redeemable ordinary shares and of purchase by a company of its own shares was introduced. This brought the UK broadly into line with practice in the USA (see TREASURY STOCK) and in continental Europe.

Even before the 1981 Act, some PREFERENCE SHARES in the UK were redeemable by the company. In order, nevertheless, to ensure the protection of creditors, when share capital is redeemed in the UK, amounts equal to the redemption payments must be transferred from distributable profits to a capital redemption reserve. This represents legally undistributable profits, though it is still part of SHAREHOLDERS' EQUITY.

Capital reserve. – a term sometimes used in the UK to refer to those accounts representing amounts which are not legally distributable by a company. Examples of such reserves are the SHARE PREMIUM account, which represents amounts paid in when shareholders bought their shares from the company; the CAPITAL REDEMPTION RESERVE which represents amounts that have been substituted for share capital when shares were redeemed from their owners by the company; and the

REVALUATION reserve which represents increases in the value of assets which have been recorded in the accounts but have not yet been realized by the sale of the assets.

These 'reserves', like all others in accounting, are not of course amounts of cash. The latter is an asset; the reserves are on the other side of a balance sheet showing, in a sense, to whom the assets belong. The reserves are part of SHAREHOLDERS' EQUITY.

The equivalent US expression is 'restricted surplus'.

Capital transfer tax. – a UK tax on the passing of wealth from one person to another during life or at death. It was introduced in 1975 to replace estate duty (or death duty), and now contains a number of exemptions based on the type of property passing, the nature of the recipient and the timing of the gift.

Cash flow. – sometimes used to refer very loosely to the amount of cash coming into or out of a business in a particular period. However, it can be used as a more precise accounting term, particularly in North America, to refer to NET INCOME with DEPRECIATION charges added back. The latter will have been deducted in the calculation of the former, but is not of course a cash payment of the period in quesiton. Thus profit plus depreciation gives an impression of cash generated by trading operations. This is not very exact, particularly because of changes in inventory (stocks) and because of outstanding credit sales and purchases which have been included in the calculation of profit but will not yet have led to cash movements. However, as a quick measure it may have its uses.

In cash flow statements, funds flow statements, STATEMENTS OF CHANGES IN FINANCIAL POSITION (US) or SOURCE AND APPLICATION OF FUNDS statements (UK), the 'cash flow' is an important opening figure.

CCA. See CURRENT COST ACCOUNTING.

Certificate of incorporation. – an essential document in the setting up of a US corporation (sometimes called 'articles of incorporation'). It is filed with the appropriate state office. It includes details of the name of the corporation, its principal office, the AUTHORIZED CAPITAL, the powers and objects of the corporation, and the names of the initial directors. The UK equivalent is the MEMORANDUM OF ASSOCIATION.

Chairman's report. – a statement in the ANNUAL REPORT of a UK company in which the chairman of the board of directors reviews the progress of the past year and the prospects for the future. It will often contain acknowledgement of support from staff, suppliers, customers or shareholders; it may make some political points about taxation, investment or inflation. The report is not a mandatory requirement, thus it neither obeys particular rules nor follows a standard format.

Chart of accounts. – a German invention that provides a detailed, standardized arrangement of account codes for assets, liabilities, capital, revenues and expenses. The system may be decimalized, and varies industry by industry. Its original purpose was to allow companies to record and prepare accounting information in a uniform, and therefore comparable, way. This would enable inter-firm comparisons, and would enhance the efficiency of industry.

Charts were imposed as a uniform system in France during World War II, and proved sufficiently successful that they were permanently adopted there as part of the *plan comptable général* (general accounting plan). Thus, throughout France, an auditor or tax inspector or industrialist can easily feel at home in a company's accounting system, because uniform coding and definitions are in use.

The chart is also the basis on which accounting information is sent annually from all companies to the Ministry of Economics and Finance. It is then collated, and can be used to assist in the planning of the economy.

In Germany, there is a voluntary chart of accounts, which is still useful for its original inter-firm comparative purposes.

Close companies. – UK companies which are controlled by their directors or by five or fewer participators or their associates (that is five or fewer shareholders or their families or partners). Such companies are likely, of course, to be small. They may have a similarity to partnerships in their management but are incorporated for legal and tax purposes.

An advantage of forming a company is that the owners can postpone receipt of the profit and thus income tax on it. This will be particularly useful when the profit would be large enough to cause high marginal rates of income tax to apply. The company is regarded as a separate taxable entity, which is why it pays corporation tax and can have retained profits on which the shareholders/owners have not yet suffered tax.

In order to control this way of postponing income tax for small owner-managed businesses, the close company provisions of corporation tax were introduced. Initially, these were important: approximately, they required that a close company should distribute half its income to its shareholders. Otherwise, the 'shortfall' of distributions was deemed to have been made for the purposes of income tax. However, in the 1980 Finance Act, 'shortfall' assessments were abolished except for investment income.

A listed company is required to note whether or not it is a close company in its ANNUAL REPORT. (See, also, the entry for COMPANIES).

Closing rate method. UK term for the normal method of FOREIGN CURRENCY TRANSLATION. The US term is current rate method.

CoCoA. – the acronym for Continuously Contemporary Accounting: a system of price change adjusted accounting developed by Professor Ray Chambers of the University of Sydney. This system is based on the selling price of assets (their NET REALIZABLE VALUE); assets and liabilities are valued in this way for inclusion in the balance sheet, and profits are measured with a related CAPITAL MAINTENANCE concept.

The CoCoA balance sheet thus represents the marketable value of the resources at the disposal of the managers. This would be a useful valuation for some purposes. Further, since all the assets would be valued at 'current cash equivalents', the proponents of CoCoA argue that it gives a more sensible total than a mixture of historical costs and current values (as in HISTORICAL COST ACCOUNTING) or a mixture of various valuation bases (as in DEPRIVAL VALUE on which CURRENT COST ACCOUNTING is based).

However, critics question the relevance of selling values for a GOING CONCERN, particularly for the shareholders of the going concern, who have no power to sell its assets. In particular, the relevance of the sometimes very low selling value of plant and machinery that has just been bought and installed may be questioned. Some critics think that the system cannot cope with these problems, and that CoCoA dissolves in hot water! Perhaps for these reasons, it has not been adopted in any country. However it remains, at the very least, an elegant theory.

Commission des Opérations de Bourse (COB). – the approximate French equivalent of the SECURITIES AND EXCHANGE COMMISSION (SEC) of the USA. It was founded in 1968 by the French Government and charged with supervising and improving the financial capital market. As with all continental European bourses, there are relatively few shares listed on the Paris Bourse (about 600; see STOCK EXCHANGES). The government and banks are important providers of finance in France.

Perhaps the most obvious impact that the COB has had on the financial reporting of French listed companies results from its campaign in favour of CONSOLIDATED FINANCIAL STATEMENTS. Consolidation was virtually unknown in France in 1968, but a majority of French listed companies prepared consolidated statements by the time it became compulsory for them in 1985. When the seventh DIRECTIVE OF THE EEC is implemented, towards 1990, consolidation will be extended to far more French companies as a legal requirement.

Commissione Nazionale per le Società e la Borsa (CONSOB). – the approximate Italian equivalent of the SECURITIES AND EXCHANGE COMMISSION (SEC) in the USA. It was founded in 1974, and has pushed accounting for listed companies towards ANGLO-SAXON ACCOUNTING.

Common stock. – US term for the ordinary shares in a corporation. Normally a majority of the ownership capital will comprise issues of common stock, though PREFERENCE/PREFERRED SHARES are also issued. Stock usually has a PAR VALUE, which is little more than a label for the type of stock. The amount that would have to be paid for one share will be determined, in the case of a listed share, by the daily price on the STOCK EXCHANGE. The total of common stock is part of the SHARE-HOLDERS' FUNDS of a company. The return to common stock is a dividend. In the long run, the size of dividends depends on the profitability of the company.

Companies. – businesses that are legal entities separate from their owners, the shareholders. Thus, companies can own assets, they can sue and be sued at law, they can have 'perpetual succession' (that is, there need be no limit to their lives, irrespective of the lives of, or changes to, the owners). Also, most companies have limited liability; to be more exact the owners of the company have limited liability for the debts of the company. In effect, the owners' liability is usually limited to their shareholdings. Because owners may be granted limited liability (in the case of the UK, from the 1855 Companies Act onwards), many investors are prepared to risk their money and become co-owners. This enables very large amounts of capital to be raised, and therefore makes very large companies possible. If there were no limited liability (as with partnerships) it would be much more difficult to persuade investors to become co-owners, without their insisting on becoming co-managers so that they could safeguard their own investments and potential liabilities. Most investors have no desire to become co-managers of businesses, and most businesses have no desire for vast numbers of co-managers. Thus, limited liability is essential for large businesses.

In the UK, before the 1844 Act it had been necessary to have an Act of Parliament or a Royal Charter in order to set up a company. Now companies are commonplace in the UK and throughout the world. They are set up with a series of legal transactions and registration with government (or state government) offices. In the UK, the MEMOR-ANDUM and ARTICLES OF ASSOCIATION outline the rules of the company; in the USA the analogous documents are the CERTIFICATE OF INCORPOR-ATION and the BYLAWS.

Throughout much of the western developed world (though not in the USA) the law distinguishes between private companies and public companies. The table below gives abbreviated designations which will be seen as part of the names of companies.

Abbreviated Company Names

	Private	Public
France	Sàrl	SA
Italy	Srl	SpA
Netherlands	BV	NV
UK	Ltd	plc
USA	--------- Inc, Ltd --------	
W Germany	GmbH	AG

It is necessary for a company to be public in order for there to be a market in its securities (shares or loans). The extreme example of a public market is a STOCK EXCHANGE listing. Thus, public companies tend to be larger than private companies. The law imposes greater restrictions on public companies. In the UK, for example, public companies must have a minimum issued capital of £50,000. The definition of DISTRIBUTABLE PROFIT is stricter for them. They are not allowed the exemptions from publication granted to certain private companies.

There are about 5,000 public companies in the UK; about half of them listed. There are about 900,000 private companies. In some countries, like West Germany and the Netherlands, public companies are required to have two-tier boards, comprising a supervisory board (containing some employee representation) and a management board. Proposals like this are contained in the draft fifth DIRECTIVE OF THE EEC.

In the USA, there is no such legal distinction between public and private. However, the analogous companies to public ones are those that are registered with the SECURITIES AND EXCHANGE COMMISSION (SEC). Companies must register with the SEC in order for there to be a market in their securities. The SEC lays down audit and disclosure requirements. Further, it provides the backing for ACCOUNTING STANDARDS. Thus, the rules for registered companies are greatly more extensive than those for unregistered companies.

See, also, CLOSE COMPANIES, PUBLIC COMPANY, PRIVATE COMPANY and CORPORATION TAX.

Company law/companies acts. In some countries, like WEST GERMANY, company law has been the main source of general and detailed requirements in accounting. In other countries, like the USA, there is virtually nothing on accounting in state or federal law; instead accounting rules are set by the SEC, by the profession, or by some combination. In the UK, before the EEC's FOURTH DIRECTIVE led to the provisions of the 1981 Companies Act, there were only general requirements in the law concerning accounting. For example, proper books of account had to be kept; annual financial statements had to be audited, to be published and to give a 'TRUE AND FAIR VIEW'; and a number of detailed disclosures had to be made.

In the UK, company law really began with the 1844 Act which enabled companies to be easily formed, and the 1855 Act which allowed LIMITED LIABILITY. Compulsory independent audit for banks followed in 1879; and for all limited companies in 1900. Not until the 1929 Act did profit and loss accounts become compulsory. Group accounts were required by the 1947 Act (consolidated into the 1948 Act).

Company law was consolidated again in the Companies Act of 1985. Before that, the principal Act of 1948 had been supplemented by Acts of 1967, 1976, 1980 and 1981. The 1981 Act added requirements for the formats of the BALANCE SHEET and the PROFIT AND LOSS ACCOUNT; extended disclosure requirements; provided certain exemptions from

publication for smaller PRIVATE COMPANIES; and introduced detailed compulsory ACCOUNTING PRINCIPLES. Many of these provisions came, via the fourth Directive, from German law (particularly the public companies law of 1965).

On several matters other than accounting, UK law has traditionally been fairly detailed. For example there are many provisions on audit, directors' duties, rights of shareholders and creditors, conduct of AGMs, and so on. The law also contains many provisions on business names and INSIDER DEALING.

Conceptual framework. – a theoretical structure to underlie the technical rules in accounting. Some accountants regard this as the equivalent of the holy grail. Members of accounting standards setting bodies are seen as searching for this mystical object, which is believed to contain the answer to 'the meaning of life, the universe and everything'.

Perhaps the best way to explain the idea of a conceptual framework is to refer to the efforts of the FINANCIAL ACCOUNTING STANDARDS BOARD (FASB) in the USA, which began a conceptual framework project after the Trueblood Committee Report of 1973 criticized the *ad hoc* nature of accounting standards. The project has led to several 'Statements of Financial Accounting Concepts'. The first statement concerned the objectives of financial statements. It was concluded that the most important aim was to provide shareholders with useful information for making financial decisions. Then, the 'elements' of financial statements were identified and defined. For example, assets, liabilities and income were discussed. These are, of course, very difficult to define with precision.

The third statement concerned the qualitative characteristics of accounting information. In order to achieve the desired objectives, it was concluded that relevance and reliability were the two most important features. 'Relevance' would be determined with respect to the decisions to be made by users; 'reliability' would increase with objectivity.

It seems obvious, at least to academic accountants, that before one makes rules in accounting, one should find out who uses the information and what they want or are likely to understand. Thus, this effort seems long overdue. However, criticism has come from some practitioners that the search is too expensive and theoretical. Also, some academics think that the setting of ACCOUNTING STANDARDS is bound to be a 'political' process involving company managers, auditors and governments. Thus, an effective conceptual framework which really reduces arguments about which rules must be followed is unlikely to be found. It is feared that the arguments will merely move back to the determination of the framework itself.

Nevertheless, it may be that it would be more difficult for interest groups to argue against *parts* of the conceptual framework, and that some existing accounting practices would become difficult to defend.

In the UK, a small amount of attention has been paid to the need for a conceptual framework. However, the idea that accounting standards should make a coherent package with a solid theoretical basis has not caught on amongst a pragmatic profession, some members of which are largely uneducated in aspects of accounting other than the technical.

Conservatism. – the fundamental and ancient accounting concept that accountants should, when in doubt, show the worse picture rather than the better. Conservatism requires that assets should be shown at the lowest of all reasonable values; that all foreseeable losses should be accounted for immediately, but that profits should never be recorded until they become REALIZED PROFITS. Thus, conservatism tends to cause assets and profits to be understated.

The cause of this convention of caution is said to be that the accountant has been expected to provide the counterweight to the natural optimism of entrepreneurs. Thus, the end result is more reliable for creditors or outside shareholders. In UK accounting standards (SSAP 2) and company law, the concept is required under the name of 'prudence'. This latter word is sometimes used to imply a somewhat more flexible attitude than strict conservatism.

Examples of the effect of conservatism on detailed accounting practices would be the 'lower of cost and market' rule in the valuation of INVENTORIES (stocks), and the tendency to treat many costs as expenses immediately even though they may have future benefits, like advertising and research expenditure.

Some accountants think that conservatism is overdone. Obviously it can be taken so far that the accounting figures become misleadingly low. They would then lose both relevance and reliability which may be seen as important features of accounting information (see CONCEPTUAL FRAMEWORK).

Consistency. – the concept that a company should use the same rules of measurement and valuation from year to year in its financial statements. This is now well established in most developed countries. A company may be allowed to change in special circumstances, like an alteration in ACCOUNTING STANDARDS, but the change should always be disclosed in the annual report. The purpose of consistency is to enable a better comparison of a year's profits and value with those of previous years. The concept that different *companies* should use the same rules to assist inter-company comparisons might be called UNIFORMITY.

Consistency is required in the UK by accounting standards (SSAP 2) and by company law. In the USA, the auditors' report contains a statement that accounting principles have been consistently applied.

Consolidated financial statements. – a means of presenting the position and results of a parent and its subsidiary companies as if they were a single entity. Consolidation ignores the separation of parents and subsidiaries due to legal and geographical factors; it accounts for the group of companies as a single entity. Approximately, the financial statements of all the companies in the group are added together, with adjustments to extract intra-group trading and indebtedness, as explained below.

The purpose of this technique, which is standard practice throughout the Anglo-Saxon world, is to show existing and potential investors the state of affairs and success of the total business that is owned by the shareholders. Consolidation became popular in the USA well before 1920 and in the UK shortly afterwards. However, it is still not normal for most of continental Europe. There are several factors that may explain this difference. First, 'big business' and group structures were and are more common in the English-speaking world. Secondly, a new practice like consolidation needs an inventive and powerful accountancy profession to bring it about, and a law which is permissive enough to allow it to develop. These conditions existed in the USA and the UK, but not in most of continental Europe.

The third factor behind the development of consolidation was the needs of private shareholders, who wanted an overall view of the group of companies that they owned. By contrast, the main users of accounting in some continental countries are bankers, governments and tax authorities. Some bankers regard consolidated financial statements as misleading because they disguise the legal indebtedness of particular companies – one cannot sue a *group* for debt, only particular companies. Similarly, the tax authorities in most countries assess individual companies not consolidated groups. In countries like France, where the government uses accounting in order to assist in the control of the economy, the consolidation methods of accountants merely confuse the issue, as the government will have its own national consolidation techniques.

In the UK, the 1947 Companies Act was the first strong provision calling for 'group accounts', although other methods than consolidation were possible. This was supplemented by ACCOUNTING STANDARDS (SSAP 14) which lay down more detail and call for consolidation in most cases. In the USA, various professional opinions and standards cover consolidation (e.g. APB Opinion 16). In EEC countries, consolidation will become compulsory on the implementation of the seventh DIRECTIVE on company law of 1983. Suitable national laws are to be in effect by 1990.

The main technique of consolidation (called acquisition accounting, group accounting or full consolidation) is used when a parent owns more than 50 per cent of the shares of another company (the subsidiary). Since this normally means full *control*, 100 per cent of the assets, liabilities, revenues and expenses of the subsidiary are added together with the parent's on a line by line basis. Thus, the cash or the sales shown in the consolidated (or group) financial statements will be the total cash or sales of the group of companies. However, the investment by the parent in the subsidiary is intra-group. Thus, the parent company's investment (an asset) is cancelled against the subsidiary's share capital and reserves (on the capital and liabilities side of its balance sheet). If the parent owns less than 100 per cent of the shares, this will affect the calculation, and a 'minority interest' will be shown on the capital and liabilities side of the group's balance sheet. Further, the cost of the investment often exceeds the capital of the subsidiary; in such cases GOODWILL on consolidation arises and may be shown as an asset in the group balance sheet.

In years subsequent to the initial acquisition, these cancellations are not recalculated (at least not in ANGLO-SAXON ACCOUNTING). Any profits earned are recorded as group profit, which affects group reserves in the balance sheet, after deduction of any share due to minority interests.

The group sales, profit and other revenues or expenses are reduced to the extent that amounts are passing between group companies. Otherwise, goods sold from one subsidiary to another and then sold to outside customers would be double-counted. Also, any indebtedness from one group company to another is cancelled out as part of the process of consolidation. A further series of complicated consolidation adjustments is necessary when a subsidiary's financial statements are expressed in a different currency from its parent's; FOREIGN CURRENCY TRANSLATION is then necessary.

Not all business combinations are accounted for as acquisitions; some are dealt with by a method called POOLING OF INTERESTS (US) or MERGER ACCOUNTING (UK). This leads to a somewhat different technique of consolidation, which normally results in more attractive figures. It is a method which has been more widely used in the USA than elsewhere.

A further aspect of consolidated financial statements is that they include a partial form of consolidation for those companies over which a company exercises significant influence; normally this means JOINT VENTURES or companies held between 20 and 50 per cent. These are called ASSOCIATED COMPANIES in the UK, and a description of the normal Anglo-Saxon practice for them can be found under that heading.

Some *subsidiaries* are excluded from full consolidation but treated as associated companies because they are very different from other parts of the group or because control is restricted, for example by an overseas government. In the USA in particular, financial institution subsidiaries are excluded from non-financial groups because such companies are so different from the others that the group picture might be misleading.

There are yet other different treatments which should be mentioned. A method popular in France for joint ventures is PROPORTIONAL CONSOLIDATION, whereby only the appropriate proportion (depending on the parent's holding) of the joint venture's assets, liabilities, etc are brought into the group's financial statements.

Lastly, for holdings of less than 20 per cent, the group balance sheet will show just the cost of the investment, and the only income recognized will be the dividends from the company. Such a holding is sometimes called a 'trade investment' if it is long-term.

In the USA, a company which has subsidiaries or associated companies would present only consolidated financial statements. In the UK, a company's annual report also contains a balance sheet of the parent company alone, showing subsidiaries, etc as investments at cost. This might be regarded as somewhat archaic and confusing.

Constant dollar accounting. – an alternative name for a system of inflation accounting which adjusts financial statements for the change in a general prices index. See GENERAL PURCHASING POWER ACCOUNTING.

Consultative Committee of Accountancy Bodies (CCAB). – set up by the six professional accountancy bodies in the British Isles after proposals for their merger failed in 1970. These bodies, in order of size, are:

	Designatory Letters
The Institute of Chartered Accountants in England and Wales (ICAEW)	ACA, FCA
The Chartered Association of Certified Accountants (CACA)	ACCA, FCCA
The Chartered Institute of Management Accountants (CIMA)	ACMA, FCMA
The Institute of Chartered Accountants of Scotland (ICAS)	CA
The Chartered Institute of Public Finance and Accountancy (CIPFA)	IPFA
The Institute of Chartered Accountants in Ireland (ICAI)	ACA, FCA

The founding dates (earliest predecessor bodies in brackets) and their approximate number of members are:

Body	Dates	Members (000)
ICAEW	1880 (1870)	78
CACA	1939 (1891)	26
CIMA	1919	24
ICAS	1951 (1854)	11
CIPFA	1885	9
ICAI	1888	5

The CCAB co-ordinates the rulemaking of the profession for its own members. In particular, there are two very important committees, called the ACCOUNTING STANDARDS COMMITTEE (ASC) and the AUDITING PRACTICES COMMITTEE (APC). The ASC sets the detailed technical rules of valuation and measurement to be used by accountants when preparing annual accounts and audit opinions on them. These rules, called Accounting Standards, supplement the Companies Act and are an attempt partially to define a 'TRUE AND FAIR VIEW'. The APC deals with the standard procedures to be followed by auditors. The figure below shows a diagrammatic view of these institutions.

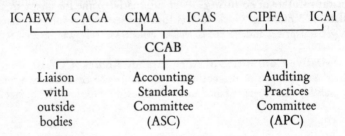

Contingent liabilities. – possible future liabilities. As part of CONSERVATISM, accountants recognize all reasonably probable losses in advance. However, some losses are merely 'possible' and are contingent upon some event, like the loss of a law case or a debtor defaulting on a BILL OF EXCHANGE which the company has guaranteed. These 'contingencies' are not accounted for, in the sense of adjusting the financial statements, but are added to the notes to the BALANCE SHEET. A suitable note will explain the cause of the contingency and the amount (or an estimate). Instructions on practice are contained in ACCOUNTING STANDARDS: SSAP 18 in the UK and SFAS 5 in the USA.

Convertible loan stock. – long-term debts/DEBENTURES/bonds that are convertible, at some future date at the option of the lender, into equity, i.e. ordinary shares (UK)/common stock (US), of the borrowing company. This means that investors can have the safety of debt finance (in that there is fixed annual interest, and preferential repayment of capital if a company is wound up), with the profit-sharing aspects of equity if the company does well. For the company, the advantages are that it will be easier to attract finance at a reasonable annual cost of capital, and that the returns to the providers of finance will initially be in the form of interest, which is tax-deductible.

The legal documents drawn up for the issue of the convertible stock will specify the dates between which conversion is possible, the number of shares to be received in exchange for a certain amount of loan stock, and the rate of interest and redemption date of the loan stock (if unconverted).

Corporation tax. In the UK, corporation tax was introduced in 1965 as a separate tax on companies. Before that, companies paid income tax on their business profits (as sole traders and partners still do) plus a special profits tax. In the USA, companies still pay 'income tax'.

Such taxes vary in three main ways. First, the rates are different from year to year and from country to country. The full rate in the UK is 35% of taxable income for 1986, but there is a 30% rate for companies earning below a certain amount. In the USA, as for persons, the corporate income tax is paid in increasing marginal rate bands.

Secondly, the definition of taxable income also varies. In some countries, like France or West Germany, taxable income is very closely related to accounting net profit. In ANGLO-SAXON ACCOUNTING countries, the calculation of taxable income starts with accounting net profit but may involve several adjustments. Perhaps the greatest number of potential adjustments exist in the UK. For example, accounting DEPRECIATION is disallowed; instead a uniform and generous tax depreciation system is granted, called CAPITAL ALLOWANCES. There are, also, many other expenses added back to accounting net profit: general provisions for BAD DEBTS; fines; non-trading expenses like political donations; and potentially extravagant expenses like entertaining UK customers.

INTEREST payments can be deducted for both accounting and tax purposes, but DIVIDENDS are not deductible for either purpose. Dividends received from other companies have been paid out of taxed corporate income; in the UK these are called FRANKED INVESTMENT INCOME and are not taxed again to corporation tax. In some other countries, including the USA, they are fully or partially taxed. In the UK there are also some adjustments for financial receipts and payments (like interest), which are treated on the MATCHING basis for accounting, but are treated on a cash received or cash paid basis for taxation.

Thirdly, tax systems differ in their treatment of dividends. The main systems in use in the developed western world are called the 'classical' system and the 'imputation' system. The former is used, for example, in the USA, the Netherlands, Luxembourg and Australia. It is a system which treats the company and its shareholders as fully separate taxable entities. Thus dividends, which are paid out of taxed corporate income, are then brought fully in to charge to personal income tax in the hands of the shareholder recipients. This 'double taxation' might seem somewhat unfair compared to the single burden of tax on partnerships. Also, it may discourage the payments of dividends, which would not enable shareholders to re-channel profits to those companies which are seen as most profitable.

In order to reduce these problems, the 'imputation system' has been adopted in the UK (in 1973) and in most other EEC countries. Such

'Dammit Sam I expect my accountant to contribute a bit more than — "it's a fair cop"'

systems wholly or partially impute to the shareholders some of the corporation tax paid by the companies on the income out of which dividends are paid. The mechanism for imputation is a 'tax credit', given to the shareholders at the time of a dividend. This is related in size to the dividend, and can be used in full or partial 'payment' of individual income tax liability. In the UK, the tax credit is linked to the basic rate of income tax. For example, when that rate is 29 per cent, the tax credit is 29/71. This means that basic rate taxpayers end up by paying no personal income tax on the dividends.

Corporate income taxes may have many effects on the decisions of companies. For example, they may lead to a bias in favour of loan finance, which is tax deductible; they may lead to more investment, because of generous tax depreciation allowances.

Usually there are, also, complicated provisions with respect to the set-off of losses. In the UK, they can be carried back to some extent against past profits, and carried forward without limit. Some other countries are less generous.

The Corporate Report. – a report published in 1975 by a working party of the UK ACCOUNTING STANDARDS COMMITTEE. It was designed to investigate the users of published financial statements and their information needs. A fairly lengthy list of users was recognized, including shareholders, creditors, customers, suppliers and employees. The qualitative characteristics of financial statements deemed desirable for them included relevance, objectivity, timeliness, completeness, reliability and understandability. This also led to several suggestions for extra reports, for example VALUE ADDED STATEMENTS.

Criticisms of the report include that it was based on *assumptions* about who the users of financial statements are and what they need, rather than on research. Further, the list of characteristics may not be helpful in choosing between alternative accounting rules or presentations, because the characteristics are vague and contradictory. For example, completeness seems to be inconsistent with timeliness and understandability.

In the USA the search for a CONCEPTUAL FRAMEWORK has been much more lavish.

Cost. Valuation practices in many countries are based on HISTORICAL COST, that is the purchase price or production cost of assets. INVENTORIES (stocks) are valued at the 'lower of cost or market'. OIL AND GAS ACCOUNTING is often based on a 'full cost' method. Cost can also be used to mean CURRENT REPLACEMENT COST.

The profit of a business is calculated by setting the costs (or EX-PENSES) of the period against its revenues.

There are also many ways of analysing costs for COST ACCOUNTING or MANAGEMENT ACCOUNTING purposes.

Cost accounting. – the breaking down of various costs and revenues by product, location or manager. The purpose is to assist managers in working out which is the most profitable product, or which is the cheapest location, or how much should be charged for particular products. One of the most difficult problems is the allocation of costs which are joint for several 'cost centres'. Such costs may be called overheads or indirect costs, like property taxes or supervisory staff. Some of these are fixed and some are variable. Some are controllable by particular managers and some are not. Decision making may be aided by leaving out of account the fixed and uncontrollable costs.

Cost of sales. – the costs associated with making the products that have been sold in a period. This includes the appropriate proportions of production overheads, but not administration expenses. It excludes the costs of unsold production. The cost of sales is deducted from the sales revenue of the period in order to calculate gross profit from trading.

The cost of sales is not the same as the purchases of materials for the period for two reasons. First, inventories (stocks) may have been built up or reduced during the period; secondly, work will probably have been carried out on the inventories during the period. Thus, the cost of sales includes the factory wages and overheads.

In order to adjust for inventory changes, the calculation of the cost of sales is: opening inventory (stock) *plus* purchases of materials *less* closing inventory (stock). However, during periods of rising prices, the increase in value of the closing inventory may not be fully associated with a physical increase. Thus, there are HOLDING GAINS. For tax purposes, reductions in taxable income have sometimes been arranged for this (allowance of LIFO in the USA, and use of STOCK RELIEF in the UK). For INFLATION ACCOUNTING purposes, a COST OF SALES ADJUST-MENT is used (see below).

Cost of sales adjustment (COSA). – an amount used, in various systems of INFLATION ACCOUNTING, to adjust the COST OF SALES for the extent to which its components have been affected by price changes. The calculation of the cost of sales includes the opening and closing inventory figures. The former will have been determined using inventory prices ruling before the beginning of the year, and the latter using prices of before the end of the year. However, the purchases figure will normally be composed of various prices that amount to an average for the year. Thus several different price levels are involved in the cost of sales, and the result is that the calculation does not give a good picture of the *current* cost of sales.

The COSA is designed to correct for this. It is calculated by adjusting opening and closing inventory (and purchases, if necessary) to average-for-the-year prices. When prices are rising, the current cost of sales will be larger than the unadjusted cost of sales, so the differences (the COSA) will be an extra charge (a DEBIT) against profit. Thus profit, adjusted for the COSA, will be smaller when prices are rising.

Under GENERAL PURCHASING POWER systems, the adjustments will use a general prices index. Under CURRENT VALUE systems, the inventory prices (or an index of them) will be used. For tax purposes, some analogous adjustments are allowed: in the USA, companies are allowed to adopt LIFO for all purposes (which has a somewhat similar effect in many cases); and in the UK, there was a special system of STOCK RELIEF.

In some sense, the unadjusted profit has been made. The problem is that, if the business is to maintain the same level of inventories, some of its profit is tied up in those inventories. A numerical example will help. Suppose that inventory cost 100; and that it was sold for 160, when its replacement cost was 150. HISTORICAL COST ACCOUNTING profit is given by:

	Cost	100
+	Profit	60
	Sale	160

However, a more useful view might be:

	Cost	100
+	Holding gain	50
	Replacement cost	150
+	Operating profit	10
	Sale	160

Whether one regards the profit as '10', '60' or some other figure depends upon one's concept of CAPITAL MAINTENANCE. However, the extra information in the second sum should be useful anyway. In the above case, with only one purchase or one opening inventory, the COSA is also the HOLDING GAIN.

Creative accounting. There is a well-known story about a large company that was interviewing several applicants for a senior accounting job. The applicants were given masses of accounting data and asked to calculate the profit. The applicant who got the job was the one who asked: 'What profit had you in mind?'. There are so many subjective elements in the measurement of value or profit, that a wide range of answers is often legal and in conformity with GENERALLY ACCEPTED ACCOUNTING PRINCIPLES. Thus, there is the opportunity to be 'creative'.

A rather more old-fashioned, similar expression is 'window-dressing'. It was concern along these lines that helped to lead to the establishment of the bodies that set ACCOUNTING STANDARDS.

Credit. This word has two general meanings, though they both come from the same root. The origin is that *credit* is the Latin for 'he believes' or 'he trusts'. When the only accounting records of a business were those of people who owed the business money, or were owed money by it, the simple entries would have been *debit* for 'he owes' and *credit* for 'he trusts' or *is* owed. Thus a creditor is someone who is owed money.

As record-keeping developed into DOUBLE ENTRY, a debit and a credit were invented for all transactions. Thus, for example, a purchase of raw materials from a supplier who is not yet to be paid is recorded as: *debit* purchases; *credit* the supplier (the creditor). Similarly, a sale to a customer who is not yet to pay cash is recorded as: *debit* the customer (the debtor); *credit* sales. In the full system, any increase in revenues, liabilities or capital is a credit entry, as is any decrease in assets or expenses. If the system is working properly, the total of all the debits will equal the total of all the credits.

The credit side of an ACCOUNT is conventionally the right hand side. This may be because, historically, creditors were regarded as 'good' because they trusted one; and the right hand has always been regarded as the 'good' side (for sheep instead of goats, for the 'good' thief to be crucified on, for the important guest at the side of the host, etc).

The other meaning of credit is closely connected. To 'extend credit' or to 'make sales on credit' is to trust another person. The lender becomes the creditor, that is the one who trusts.

Creditors. As explained under CREDIT, a creditor is a 'truster', someone to whom a business owes money. The US expression is ACCOUNTS PAYABLE. Creditors are created by purchases 'on credit' or loans of various sorts. Short-term creditors are included under 'current liabilities' on a balance sheet; they are expected to be paid within the year. If credit purchases are the cause, the title used might be 'trade creditors'.

Long-term creditors are those who are not expected to be paid within the year. These might be trade creditors but would more likely be holders of bonds or DEBENTURES. The latter would normally be entitled to receive interest, whereas trade creditors are not. However, trade creditors often offer discounts for prompt payment, which is an implied way of charging interest.

Creditors of all sorts are shown in a balance sheet at the amounts which a business expects to pay. Particularly in the case of long-term loans, this may be different from the amount originally borrowed or from the amount that would have to be paid to redeem the loan at the balance sheet date (see DEBENTURES).

Cum dividend. A share is bought cum dividend (or cum div) if the purchaser would receive the next payment of dividend. This is normal. The opposite is *ex dividend*, which may apply for a short period around the dividend date. In this case, the seller intends to keep the next dividend, presumably to be received soon.

Cumulative preference shares. – the normal type of PREFERENCE SHARES, on which any arrears of dividends have to be settled before the ordinary shareholders can be paid a dividend.

Currency translation. – see FOREIGN CURRENCY TRANSLATION.

Current assets. By convention, an ASSET on a BALANCE SHEET is 'current' if it is expected to change its form within a year from the balance sheet date. Such assets include inventories (stocks), accounts receivable (US)/debtors (UK), and cash. Also, a balance sheet may include current asset investments; that is, those designed to be held for a short period. The 'one year' convention is a rule of thumb for the more fundamental distinction between those assets that are to continue to be used in the business (FIXED ASSETS) and assets that are part of circulating or trading capital. Thus, just as investments can be fixed or current, so automobiles can be fixed (if part of a fleet of company cars) or current (if part of the trading inventory of a car dealer).

Strictly, one need not expect a current asset to turn into *cash* within the year, but to *circulate*, as stated above. For example, inventory might be expected to be sold to credit customers, which would delay the receipt of cash.

The nearness of current assets to disposal leads to an enhanced importance of their market value (normally NET REALIZABLE VALUE). Thus although, under HISTORICAL COST ACCOUNTING, market value tends to be ignored for fixed assets, it is not ignored for current assets: first, notes to the balance sheet may show the market value of some current assets; secondly, the balance sheet valuation is carried out by using the 'LOWER OF COST AND MARKET' rule. Particularly in times of rising prices, this would normally lead to the use of historical cost. However, the implied constant reference to the possibility of a lower market value is an example of the CONSERVATISM inherent in accounting.

In UK balance sheets, current assets are shown below fixed assets, and in increasing order of liquidity (with cash last). In US balance sheets it is more normal to start with current assets.

The expression 'net current assets' (or working capital) means the current assets *less* the CURRENT LIABILITIES. A ratio of current assets to current liabilities is called a CURRENT RATIO.

Current cost accounting (CCA). – one of many possible systems designed to adjust accounting for changing prices. It is often included under the generic heading INFLATION ACCOUNTING, although it does not involve adjustments for inflation, but for specific price changes relating to the business' assets.

CCA is particularly associated with the UK, Australia and New Zealand. In the UK, a CCA system was proposed by a government committee in the Sandilands Report of 1975. This rejected the rather simple method of CURRENT PURCHASING POWER ACCOUNTING which had been preferred by the accountancy profession. However, the profession responded by setting up the Morpeth Committee which prepared a CCA Exposure Draft, ED 18, in 1976. This was voted down by the membership of the Institute of Chartered Accountants in England and Wales. It was followed by the 'Hyde' interim guidelines, by ED 24, and in 1980 by an ACCOUNTING STANDARD, SSAP 16.

SSAP 16 called for listed and other large companies either to adopt CCA for their main financial statements, or to prepare supplementary CCA statements while retaining HISTORICAL COST ACCOUNTING main statements. SSAP 16 was not generally welcomed by the profession or by companies, who looked on it as extra work and complication. However, some users were supportive of CCA, and the government has made it clear that some form of price-change accounting should be developed. Nevertheless, SSAP 16 ceased to be mandatory and had not been replaced by the end of 1986.

Balance sheets under CCA contain assets which are normally valued at net CURRENT REPLACEMENT COST. This is what it would cost to buy an identical replacement (or, if necessary, a similar replacement after adjustment for the differences). The replacement cost is reduced to the extent that the asset has been depreciated, hence 'net' current replacement cost. In practice, index numbers for a large variety of assets are available, and have been used as estimates for actual replacement costs.

It was said above that replacement cost was 'normally' used. The exact valuation method is called 'value to the business', 'value to the owner' or 'DEPRIVAL VALUE'. This method determines the value of an asset on the basis of how much worse off the business would be if it were deprived of the asset. Normally, deprival would be followed by the purchase of a replacement. However, sometimes this would be too high a value: when an asset was about to be sold and not replaced (in which case, NET REALIZABLE VALUE would be used) or when an asset was to continue in use but not to be replaced (in which case, ECONOMIC VALUE or the amount recoverable from further use would be used). Clearly, there is subjectivity in the choice of value, and then in the determination of value under any of the three methods. However, the values are likely to be more relevant than historical costs for certain decisions.

A CCA profit and loss account contains several adjustments compared to an historical cost one. There is a DEPRECIATION adjustment to reflect the fact that depreciation based on a current cost would be higher (when prices of the assets are rising), and a COST OF SALES ADJUSTMENT to recognize the effect of changing prices on inventories (stocks). However, the most controversial adjustments in CCA systems are for monetary items. In SSAP 16, there was a MONETARY WORKING CAPITAL ADJUSTMENT to take account of the effect of price changes on debtors and creditors; and a GEARING ADJUSTMENT which is an adjustment connected with the fact that the business gains at the expense of lenders when the value of money falls due to rising prices.

Current liabilities. – those amounts on a BALANCE SHEET that are expected to be paid by the business within a year. Thus they will include trade creditors (UK)/accounts payable (US), certain tax liabilities, and proposed dividends. Bank overdrafts are included on the grounds that they fluctuate in size and are technically recallable at short notice.

Current liabilities are valued at their 'face value', the amount that is expected to be paid.

In UK balance sheets, it is normal for current liabilities ('creditors falling due within one year') to be shown below the CURRENT ASSETS so that the calculation of net current assets (or working capital) can be shown.

Current assets and current liabilities are compared in the CURRENT RATIO.

Current purchasing power accounting (CPP). – a method of adjusting HISTORICAL COST ACCOUNTING financial statements to take account of inflation. CPP is the term used in the UK for the system recommended in the provisional ACCOUNTING STANDARD, PSSAP 7, of 1974 which was abandoned when the government-sponsored Sandilands Committee recommended CURRENT COST ACCOUNTING.

There are several other titles for a system like CPP, including GENERAL PURCHASING POWER ACCOUNTING; see that entry for a more detailed description.

Current rate method. – the US term for the normal method of FOREIGN CURRENCY TRANSLATION. The UK term is 'closing rate method'.

Current ratio. – the relationship between the CURRENT ASSETS and the CURRENT LIABILITIES of a business. It is a measure of liquidity that can be used when comparing one company with another or one year with another. A higher current ratio means greater liquidity and greater safety. However, it may mean that the resources of the business are inefficiently tied up in unproductive assets like cash or debtors (UK)/accounts receivable (US).

There is no 'correct' current ratio. The most sensible procedure is to view the ratio of a particular business in the context of its own industry. Retail stores are able to survive on much lower ratios than manufacturing companies which have a much slower turnover. A ratio of '2' might be high for the former and low for the latter.

For an even more short-run test of liquidity, one could calculate the QUICK RATIO, or acid test. This omits the less current assets, such as inventories (stocks).

Current replacement cost. – the amount that would have to be paid to replace an asset at any moment, including costs of purchase. Often a problem will arise in that an exact replacement is no longer available. The replacement cost of a 'modern equivalent asset' will then have to be used, adjusting for differences in the services provided. In practice, replacement costs are often estimated by the use of price indices for the particular type of asset.

Current replacement costs are used in various forms of price-change adjusted accounting, like CURRENT COST ACCOUNTING. This uses replacement costs, under *most* circumstances, for assets in the BALANCE SHEET. However, it would be possible to use only such valuations. This would be called REPLACEMENT COST ACCOUNTING, and is used to some extent in the Netherlands.

Balance sheets under these various systems will contain *net* current replacement costs; that is, after adjustment for DEPRECIATION.

Current value accounting (CVA). – a particular version of price-change adjusted accounting. Its main adjustments (from HISTORICAL COST ACCOUNTING) are for the price changes of the business' assets, not for general inflation. See INFLATION ACCOUNTING.

D

Day books. – part of the DOUBLE ENTRY bookkeeping system. They are the books of account which initially record the very frequent transactions of a business, like sales and purchases, so that the main accounting records are not swamped with masses of detail. Thus, there may be the 'sales day book', the 'purchases day book' and so on. These 'books of original entry' are totalled periodically, perhaps daily, and the totals taken to the main ACCOUNTS.

Debentures. – UK expression for certain types of long-term loans made to a company. Normally, debentures are 'secured' on the assets of the company by mortgage deeds. Thus, a debenture-holder would be able to persuade a Court to force a company to sell those assets if the company was otherwise unable to pay the interest on the debentures or unable to pay back the loan at the fixed redemption date.

The debenture deed will specify the rights of the holder, including the annual interest, redemption date, and redemption (or maturity) value. Some debentures are convertible into ordinary shares. Some are irredeemable.

The meaning of 'debenture' in the USA is a debt security which is not protected with tangible assets, but by the general credit of the issuer.

Debentures can be bought and sold after issue. The market price will depend upon the debenture's rate of interest and the market rate of interest. As the market rate rises, so the price of the debenture falls, in order that a given investment in debentures yields the market rate of interest. Of course, as the debenture approaches its maturity date, its value approaches the maturity/redemption/face value.

Debentures are part of the long-term liabilities or debt capital of a company.

Debit. The word 'debit' is naturally associated with DOUBLE ENTRY, but pre-dates it. It derives from the Latin for 'he owes'. Thus, when a merchant's only records were of the amounts owed to him and by him, the *debit* was one of the two types of record. An entry in the accounting records of 'Smith *debit* 100' merely records that Smith owes 100, perhaps for a sale to Smith without immediate receipt of cash. Similarly, CREDIT entries were those for persons who 'trusted' the business by extending credit.

As the bookkeeping system expanded, every transaction was seen to have both a debit and a credit. Thus, the above sale to Smith would be recorded as '*Debit* Smith 100; *Credit* Sales 100'. When Smith pays the 100, the entry would be '*Debit* Cash 100; *Credit* Smith 100'. Smith's debt is now cancelled.

In the full double-entry system, all increases in assets and expenses and all decreases in capital, liabilities or revenues are debits. If the recording has been done correctly, the total of the debits will always equal the total of the credits.

The debits are to be found on the left hand side of ACCOUNTS. This has always been the case, and may be due to the fact that left-handedness is regarded as 'bad' (this was the side of Judas at the Last Supper, of the goats at the Last Judgement, etc). The 'good' people who extend credit to the business are shown instead on the right. In Latin, we note, left is *sinister*.

Debtors. – by derivation, 'debitors', that is those with DEBIT balances in the books of account of a business. 'Debit', as explained in the preceding entry, means 'he owes'. In a BALANCE SHEET, debtors are usually mostly trade debtors, i.e. customers who have not yet paid cash. The US terminology is 'accounts receivable'. Such amounts are shown as CURRENT ASSETS because they are generally expected to be paid within the year.

In a balance sheet, debtors are valued at what they are expected to pay, bearing in mind the principle of CONSERVATISM. Thus, BAD DEBTS are written off, and provisions (allowances in US terminology) are made for doubtful debts. The provisions can be both specific (against suspected debts) and general (based on the average experience of bad debts).

In the UK, amounts that are expected to be paid more than one year after the balance sheet date must be mentioned in the notes to the balance sheet.

Deferred asset. – a somewhat unusual expression, referring to an asset which is neither a normal FIXED ASSET intended for continued use within the business, nor a normal CURRENT ASSET expected to change its form within the year. In the UK, the term covers amounts of recoverable ADVANCE CORPORATION TAX (ACT) that relate to the tax payable for the year beginning after the balance sheet date. Such recoverable ACT is reclaimable against corporation tax payable more than one year after the balance sheet date. Thus, it is not normally considered to be a current asset. The amount could be set off against DEFERRED TAX, but if there is insufficient for this, a deferred asset would have to be shown on the balance sheet.

Deferred tax. – caused by timing differences between when an amount is recognized for accounting income purposes and when it is recognized for taxable income. For example, suppose that depreciation for tax purposes (i.e. in the UK, CAPITAL ALLOWANCES) is more rapid than for accounting purposes; in such a case, in early years of an asset's life, tax depreciation will be larger than accounting depreciation (and vice versa later). Thus there are timing differences. They can also arise as a result of the deferring of taxation on capital gains until the gains are realized.

Such differences are usually insignificant in most continental European countries, so deferred tax is not a problem there. In some 'Anglo-Saxon' countries, the differences can be very large and can have a major effect on financial statements. Thus deferred tax accounting has been an area of considerable controversy. The basic question is whether to account fully for the deferred tax. To do so means taking a MATCHING CONCEPT approach, and acknowledging that the tax reductions in any year, due to timing differences that will reverse, really belong to future years. The payment of cash will still be delayed, but the tax charge recorded in the income statement (US)/profit and loss account (UK) will be increased to show the tax that would have been paid without the tax incentives.

Many companies find this treatment unattractive: the annual tax shown is artificially increased and a growing 'liability' is shown on the balance sheet. In the UK in the late 1970s, the combination of high inflation and generous capital allowances and STOCK RELIEF brought matters to a head. Up to that point, the Anglo-Saxon world had been fully accounting for deferred tax, for example under APB Opinion 11 in the USA, and SSAP 11 in the UK.

The very large deferred tax balances in the UK led to complaints that these amounts should not be shown on balance sheets because they were not expected to be payable in the foreseeable future, assuming the company was a going concern. Pressure from large companies brought about a change in standard practice in the UK when SSAP 15 was issued in 1978. This called for partial accounting for deferred tax; that is, only for those amounts that really are liabilities, because they are expected to be paid. UK practice is still based on this notion; and the idea is attractive to many companies in other Anglo-Saxon countries.

Perhaps the most important point is to note that a company's policy with respect to deferred tax will seriously affect its financial statements. The method used should be disclosed in a company's statement of ACCOUNTING POLICIES.

Depreciation. – a charge against the profit of a period to represent the wearing out of FIXED ASSETS in that period. So, machinery and equipment, vehicles and buildings are depreciated, though land normally is not. The technique of depreciation means that accountants do not charge the whole cost of a fixed asset against the profit of the year of purchase, but they charge it gradually over the years of the use and wearing out of the asset. This fits with the MATCHING CONCEPT.

In order to calculate depreciation, it is necessary to estimate the useful life of the asset and the scrap value, if any, at the end of that life. The way in which the net cost is depreciated over the asset's life depends upon the depreciation method chosen. Straight-line depreciation involves the allocation of the same proportion of the cost to each year of the asset's life. This is a simple and, thus, popular method. Alternatively, a declining charge for depreciation may be suitable, perhaps to make up for increasing maintenance charges. This can be arranged by writing off the same annual percentage on the 'reducing balance' of unexpired cost.

Suppose that a machine is bought for 10,000 at the beginning of year 1. It is expected to last for five years, and to have a scrap value of 1,000. The straight-line method would charge the net cost of 9,000 over five years in equal instalments of 1,800 per year. The reducing balance method would work on the gross cost and depreciate it down to the scrap value over five years, in this case at 37%:

	Gross Cost	10000	
Year 1:	37% depreciation	3700	
	balance	6300	
Year 2:	37% depreciation	2331	
	balance	3969	
Year 3:	37% depreciation	1468	
	balance	2501	
Year 4:	37% depreciation	925	
	balance	1576	
Year 5:	37% depreciation	576	
	balance	1000	= scrap value

The percentage that will achieve this in any particular case can be calculated by a fairly simple mathematical formula. The final year's depreciation is only approximately correct, due to rounding.

A declining charge can also be obtained by using the 'sum-of-years-digits' method. This adds the digits i.e., in the above example, $5 + 4 + 3 + 2 + 1 = 15$. The first year's depreciation would then be 5/15 of the net cost; the second year's would be 4/15 of the net cost, and so on. This arranges for a declining charge.

So, the main purpose of depreciation is to try to arrive at a fair charge for the use of fixed assets, and thus a fair figure for profit. This expense is matched by a reduction in the 'value' of the related asset. However, since HISTORICAL COST ACCOUNTING balance sheets do not purport to show the value of assets, depreciation must not be expected to be a system of valuation.

Furthermore, depreciation does *not* directly serve the purpose of setting up a pool of resources for the replacement of the depreciating assets. The act of depreciation has no direct effect on cash resources, present or future. However, it does reduce profit, and this may lead to lower payments of dividends, which will leave more resources in the company.

One obvious problem for depreciation is what to do when prices are rising. At first sight, if the value of an asset is rising, it might seem that it should not be depreciated. However, on closer inspection, one realizes that the asset is still wearing out. The fact that it is worn out by a certain proportion each year should perhaps lead to *larger* depreciation charges when prices are rising. Thus under various systems of INFLATION ACCOUNTING, depreciation charges are increased over the appropriate proportion of historical cost, by a 'depreciation adjustment'.

In the UK, the rules for depreciation are to be found in COMPANY LAW and in ACCOUNTING STANDARDS. Company law demands that all fixed assets with limited useful lives be depreciated. This, of course, includes buildings and any capitalized GOODWILL or DEVELOPMENT EXPENDITURE. The accounting standard, SSAP 12, gives some more detailed rules. However, there is a special treatment in SSAP 19 for INVESTMENT PROPERTIES.

In the USA the rules are similar, and are to be found in several pronouncements including ARB 43 and APB Opinion 12.

Deprival value. – the amount by which a business would be worse off if it were deprived of a particular asset. This is sometimes referred to as its 'value to the business' or 'value to the owner'. When trying to arrive at a realistic and current value of individual assets in order to present a balance sheet, this method has much to commend it. It should be said at once, however, that deprival value is *not* the conventional valuation method for financial statements; instead HISTORICAL COST ACCOUNTING is used.

Nevertheless, in the UK, Australia and New Zealand, deprival value has been a method used for supplementary financial statements designed to take the changing prices of assets into account; for example, as required for listed and large UK companies by SSAP 16 of 1980 to 1985.

The deprival value of an asset depends upon the intentions of the business that owns it. If an asset would be replaced, its deprival value is its net CURRENT REPLACEMENT COST (CRC); this would be the normal case. However, for assets that would not be replaced the deprival value would be NET REALIZABLE VALUE (NRV) if the asset was about to be sold, or ECONOMIC VALUE if it was to continue in use. An example of the latter would be an obsolete, but still used, cotton mill. It still produces worthwhile goods; it will perhaps not be replaced at all; but it is not to be sold (except for scrap when it falls to pieces). In such a case, the NRV might be very low and would not be relevant; and the CRC would be unrealistically high. Thus the amount recoverable from its future use is what would be lost if the asset were lost.

Deprival value is unpopular with some accountants because of the subjectivity involved in the choice of method; and because all three valuation bases are more subjective than an asset's historic cost.

Development expenditure. – may be distinguished from research expenditure in that the former has a practical application in mind. In the USA, research and development costs are required to be expensed (i.e. charged immediately to the income statement) under the rules in ACCOUNTING STANDARDS, SFAS 2.

In the UK, applied development expenditure may, under certain conditions, be treated as an asset (capitalized) in the BALANCE SHEET. It must then be subject to DEPRECIATION over the future periods in which the resulting revenues occur. This is designed to implement the MATCHING CONCEPT by, to some extent, overriding CONSERVATISM. However, the standard (SSAP 13) establishes some criteria in order to ensure that any capitalization is prudent. In practice, few UK companies do have development expenditure in their balance sheets.

Direct costs. – costs which can be associated with the production of particular units or types of product, such as manufacturing wages or manufacturing materials. When direct costs are compared to sales revenues, the 'contribution' of any particular product towards overheads and profit can be calculated. Such activity would be included in COST ACCOUNTING.

Directives of the EEC on company law. – blueprints for laws that must be enacted throughout the EEC. The Commission is keen to promote the ideal of the 'common market' by trying to remove the barriers to the movement of goods and services, persons and capital. One small part of this effort is the harmonization of company law and accounting, through the drafting of 'Directives' which have to be enacted in all member states. The Commission cannot promulgate a Directive; that has to be done by the Council of Ministers, on which each member state is represented.

Many provisions of the very important UK Companies Acts of 1980 and 1981 resulted from the second and fourth Directives on company law. The following table gives some information about the Directives. In many cases, Directives are compromises between the wishes of different member states, and the UK may only accept certain unpleasant changes if other member states agree to changes that are unpleasant to them; so that there is an equalization of misery throughout the EEC! However, although the progress is slow and the changes expensive to implement, some harmonization is taking place.

Company Law Directives	Draft Dates	Date Approved	UK Law	Purpose
First	1964	1968	1972	Ultra vires rules
Second	1970, 1972	1976	1980	Private and public companies, minimum capital, distributions
Third	1970, 1973, 1975	1978		Mergers
Fourth	1971, 1974	1978	1981	Formats and rules of accounting
Fifth	1972, 1983			Structure, management and audit of companies
Sixth	1978	1982		De-mergers
Seventh	1976, 1978	1983		Group accounts
Eighth	1978, 1979	1984		Auditors
Ninth	—			Group links
Tenth	1985			International mergers
Eleventh	1986			Branches

For example, the fourth Directive introduced the requirement for standardized formats for financial statements, previously lacking in several member states, including the UK, Ireland, and the Netherlands. Also, the TRUE AND FAIR VIEW has been written in as the overriding purpose of financial statements. This was not previously the case, for example, in FRANCE or WEST GERMANY.

Directors' report. – a normal part of the contents of the ANNUAL REPORT of a UK company. It contains detailed disclosures of directors' shareholdings, etc; charitable and political donations; a review of the past year and discussion of future plans; and many other matters.

The Directors' Report must be examined by the company's auditors to ensure that it is 'consistent with' the financial statements.

In the USA, there is no direct equivalent. However, similar information is to be found in the Form 10-K which SEC-registered companies must prepare (see SECURITIES AND EXCHANGE COMMISSION).

Discounted cash flow (DCF). – future cash flows, adjusted to take account of their timing. Such 'discounted' cash flows are used when making investment choices between competing projects. The most reliable method of deciding which project is best and whether any particular one is worth doing is to work out each project's NET PRESENT VALUE

(NPV) by adding up all the discounted expected net cash flows. The NPV calculation will include the outflow of the initial investment. A project with a positive NPV is worth doing; the project with the highest NPV is the best.

The reason for discounting is that if one were offered a choice between receiving a gift of money *now* or receiving the same amount in one year's time, it would normally be sensible to take the gift at once. One could invest it for a year with interest, or buy goods now instead of later, thus enjoying them for a year longer and/or avoiding a possible price rise. The discount rate will be related to, or exactly the same as, the rate of interest on borrowing or lending money.

Thus, if one wanted to know the equivalent value *today* of an amount of money to be paid or received in the future, the amount should be 'discounted'.

Discount houses. – twelve institutions in the City of London, making up the London Discount Market Association. Their job is to borrow short and lend long. This is a risky business, but the slight difference in interest rates enables a profit to be made. Further, the Bank of England guarantees to act as a 'lender of last resort'. In return, the discount houses guarantee to buy any unsold Treasury bills at the weekly sale by the Bank.

Discount rate. – either the relevant rate for discounting future inflows or outflows of cash, for a particular person or business (see DISCOUNTED CASH FLOW); or the rate at which DISCOUNT HOUSES or other banks can borrow from the central bank.

Distributable profits and reserves. Normally, these expressions should be understood in a legal context. In general the profits of this year, plus previous years' undistributed profits, are legally available for payment as dividends. Of course, whether they *are* so distributed will depend upon the company's need for investment funds, its available cash resources and so on.

In the UK, there is an apparently simple definition for all companies: accumulated realized profits, less accumulated realized losses (see REALIZED PROFITS). The law makes it clear that this is to be interpreted in the context of strict HISTORICAL COST ACCOUNTING. If, for example, any fixed assets have been revalued, with subsequent extra depreciation charges, the legally distributable profit will be different from that in the BALANCE SHEET. For PUBLIC COMPANIES, there is a slightly more restrictive definition, based on the sufficiency of NET ASSETS compared to distributable profits.

In the USA, depending upon in which state a company is incorporated, the legally distributable profits (unrestricted earnings) will depend upon an 'earned surplus' or a 'net assets' rule (or both) similar to those above.

Dividends. – the return to shareholders, the owners of companies. Unlike INTEREST, which is a return to lenders, dividends do not have to be paid; they can be forgone for many years if the company deems this suitable for liquidity, expansion, tax saving or other reasons. Further, dividends are not at a fixed percentage, except for preference (UK)/preferred (US) shares. If a company does very well, the shareholders will benefit by higher dividends, sooner or later.

Dividends, being a return to the owners, or an 'appropriation' rather than an expense, are not charged in the calculation of profit, nor are they tax deductible for the paying company. When received by individuals, they are subject to income tax. However, this is mitigated in the USA by an annual exemption of a fixed amount of such receipts, and in the UK by a system of tax credits (see CORPORATION TAX).

Dividend cover. – the number of times that the most recent annual dividend could have been paid out of the most recent profit. It gives an indication of how secure the future dividend payments are; a high cover suggests room for contingencies.

Dividend yield. – the most recent total annual dividend per share divided by the market price. This is an indication of the cash return that can be expected by buying a particular share. However, one should remember that the shareholders also benefit from undistributed profits, since these increase the value of their company, and will lead to future dividends or capital gains.

Double entry. – a system of bookkeeping that records two aspects of every transaction. It is an Italian invention, that gradually became fully developed in the northern city states in the fourteenth century, probably in response to substantial increases in the complexity of business; particularly the extensive trading on credit, foreign branches and joint venture trading. Systems of single entry had been used for millenia. They involved the recording of cash amounts, and of debts to and from persons outside the business. An entry of DEBIT meant 'he owes', and an entry of CREDIT meant 'he trusts' (i.e. we owe him). Gradually, it became clear that every transaction could be seen to have two effects, that might both be recorded; by a debit and a credit each time. For example:

	Debit	*Credit*
A sale on account	the debt	the sale
A purchase on account	the purchase	the amount owing
A cash sale	cash	the sale
A cash purchase	the purchase	cash
Payment by an account customer	cash	cancel the debt
Payment to an account supplier	cancel the 'owing'	cash

The system has been expanded to include all possible transactions. This enables the complete recording of sales, cash, purchases, debts, various categories of expenses, etc. Each type of transaction is recorded on a separate ACCOUNT. Each account has debits on the left and credits on the right. If the bookkeeping has been done correctly, at the end of the period the total debits in the system will equal the total credits. The system is self-balancing and makes the search for errors easier. Further, a balance can be struck on an account at any time, in order to see, for example, how much cash should be present, how much any debtor owes, or how many sales there have been.

For very numerous types of transactions, like sales, there are usually 'books of original entry' (e.g. a sales DAY BOOK or a JOURNAL) that record the daily transactions, and put a summary through to the main double-entry records.

Earliest recorded use of double-entry system

At the end of an accounting period, a TRIAL BALANCE is prepared. This is a listing of all the balances on the accounts (having netted off debits against credits in each particular account). This should show equality of the total debits and total credits. The balances can then be used to prepare the financial statements. The balances for REVENUES and EXPENSES are put to a PROFIT AND LOSS ACCOUNT (UK)/INCOME STATEMENT (US); the balances for ASSETS, LIABILITIES and CAPITAL go to the BALANCE SHEET.

Double taxation. 'Double taxation' has two meanings. The most common concerns the taxation of income by the Revenue Authorities of two different countries: a particularly sad fate that befalls many companies and individuals that operate internationally. Often income arises in one country but belongs to a taxpayer resident in another. So, two governments feel that they deserve a 'slice of the action'. Fortunately, governments have realized that this is unfair and commercially inefficient. In many cases, there are 'double tax treaties' between pairs of countries to mitigate the problem. If the worst comes to the worst, a country will normally at least allow foreign taxes paid as a deduction against taxable incomes.

The other meaning of 'double taxation' relates to systems of taxation of the income of companies. Most such systems involve at least some extent of taxing corporate income twice: once in the hands of the company and then again in the hands of shareholders as recipients of dividends. This may be called the 'economic double taxation' of dividends (see CORPORATION TAX).

E

Earnings. – a technical accounting term, meaning the amount of profit (normally for a year) available to the ordinary shareholders (UK)/common stockholders (US). That is, it is the profit after all operating expenses, interest charges, taxes and dividends on preference/preferred stock. However, 'earnings' excludes EXTRA-ORDINARY ITEMS; those that are not expected to recur and are outside the normal activities of the business. Thus, the earnings figure might be taken as an estimate of sustainable profit for shareholders. In the USA, the word is also used more loosely to mean 'profit' or 'income'.

Earnings per share. – exactly what its name suggests: the most recent year's total EARNINGS divided by the number of ordinary/common shares. Of course, there can be complications, for example when the number of shares has changed during the year. The main rules for calculation are to be found in SSAP 3 in the UK, and in APB 15 in the USA.

Earnings yield. – the EARNINGS PER SHARE divided by the market price. The reciprocal of this is the PRICE/EARNINGS RATIO. Such a figure will indicate the return that might be expected from an investment in the share, and will be an index of its popularity.

Economic consequences. – the possible real economic effects of particular accounting rules. Consideration of these is a relatively recent development in the setting of ACCOUNTING STANDARDS, and so far mainly in the USA, and mainly by commentators rather than standard setters.

For example, in the late 1970s, many large US companies claimed that there were bad economic consequences of the temporal method of FOREIGN CURRENCY TRANSLATION. It was claimed that, in order to present acceptable income statements, companies had to engage in economically inefficient foreign currency manoeuvres. Thus, a technical, 'paper' series of accounting adjustments was affecting real economic decisions. Similarly, some US banks claimed that they would not have lent money to the City of New York if the subsequent rules on the accounting treatment of 'troubled debt restructuring' had been in force. Lastly, some companies have claimed that they are discouraged from sensible leasing transactions because of the accounting effects (see LEASES).

Some of these claims are suspect, but the view that standard-setters ought to take economic consequences into account has been gaining in popularity. In opposition to this, other commentators compare financial reporting to map-making. They suggest that a good map is not one that tries to affect people's behaviour, but one that tells the unbiased truth.

In the long run, 'persuasive' maps would be discredited and would be neither true nor persuasive. An arguable analogy is made from maps to financial reporting, as part of the case for aiming at 'truth': an elusive concept (see CONCEPTUAL FRAMEWORK).

Economic value. – a way of valuing assets at the expected future net cash flows from them, discounted to the present. The 'discounting' is designed to adjust for the fact that present money is more valuable than the same physical amount of future money (see DISCOUNTED CASH FLOW).

There can be little doubt that this is in some sense 'correct' but, like many of the concepts of economics, it is strong on theory but weak on practicality. As a general basis for valuing assets in a balance sheet, it is a non-starter; the problem being that values reported to outsiders (like shareholders) need to be reliable, objective and auditable. The economic value of an asset rests upon the prediction of all the future cash flows coming from it, and upon an estimation of the appropriate DISCOUNT RATE. This is far too subjective for financial reporting purposes, though the concept does appear as part of the DEPRIVAL VALUE concept used in special cases, and often without discounting, in systems of CURRENT COST ACCOUNTING.

A further problem with economic value is that it will probably be practically impossible to estimate the cash flows *from any particular asset*, since groups of assets work together to produce products and cash flows. The value of the output of a machine depends upon other machines around it, and upon the factory that it works in.

However, for *internal* investment appraisal purposes, when one has to deal with the future and with subjectivity, economic values or NET PRESENT VALUE is of great use.

EEC Accountants Study Group. – a group of accountants, from the professional bodies of the EEC, that advises the EEC Commission on company law harmonization. See GROUPE D'ETUDES DES EXPERTS COMPTABLES DE LA CEE and DIRECTIVES OF THE EEC.

Efficient market hypothesis. – an elegant and important theory, usually applied to the price of shares on large stock exchanges, that all publicly available information is immediately taken into account in the price of shares. In markets like the New York or London Stock Exchanges there are many buyers and sellers of shares, the prices are well known, and much other information is freely available. In such cases, one would expect that new relevant information about a company would very rapidly affect its price. For example, a discovery of oil by Shell or a major stoppage at General Motors or the announcement of half-yearly profit figures by IBM would be expected to affect share prices. Of course, it is only the 'new' information which would affect prices. When a company's annual report is published, it may have no effect because of prior press releases. Even the press releases may have no effect because of the widespread ability of brokers and newspapers to predict profits approximately.

From this comes the frequent, but apparently curious, spectacle of share prices *falling* when high profits are announced, or vice versa. This is caused by the fact that even higher profits had been predicted. These predictions had led to a demand for the shares, which led to a price rise.

If it really is the case that all publicly available information is immediately included into share prices, a number of startling implications follow. First, it is normally impossible to out-guess the market. That is, one cannot usefully examine company accounts and other publicly available information in order to work out which shares are better value than others. The 'market' will have worked out which look good, and will have pushed the price up until they are no longer 'good value'. In order to make money consistently as a trader, one must have insider (private) information. Thus, a normal investor might as well not waste time in analysing accounts; he should merely decide whether his personal position warrants high-dividend shares, risky shares, oil shares etc. This will depend on his tax position, his attitude to risk, and his existing portfolio. This also implies that the average published share tip will not work, after any initial price reaction due to the tip itself.

Secondly, it suggests that attempts to make profits or assets look larger or smaller by the adoption of different disclosed accounting policies will not affect share prices. The rules of accounting and auditing (see ACCOUNTING STANDARDS) should ensure disclosure of practice and of changes in practices. There should be sufficient investors, brokers, journalists, etc capable of interpreting the effects of policy changes, that share prices will be immune to them. Thus, WINDOW-DRESSING or CREATIVE ACCOUNTING should not work for listed companies.

There is considerable evidence, especially from the USA, that large stock exchanges *are* fairly efficient markets in the above sense. However, very few companies, investors, brokers, etc behave as if they are. Of course, the efficiency of the market depends upon buyers and sellers behaving as if it were *not* efficient! Efficiency depends upon all the analysis being done and the information being produced.

Employee reporting. – telling the employees how the company is performing, with the aid of specially designed annual reports. This has become much more common recently, particularly in the UK, probably because moral and commercial reasons have led to a feeling that employees should be more informed and involved in companies. The VREDELING DIRECTIVE seeks to institutionalize reporting to, and consulting with, employees for large EEC companies.

Employment reports. – the disclosure of information about employees in a company's ANNUAL REPORT. This has been taken furthest in France, where 'social balance sheets' have been part of reporting practice since a law of 1977 implemented the Sudreau Report. The information included concerns numbers and types of employees, pension rights, salaries and working conditions.

Entity convention, entity view. The entity convention is to view the business as separate from its owners. This is standard for accounting and, for many businesses, it is also the legal position. It enables accountants to prepare balance sheets that balance, because amounts contributed by and earned for the owners can be shown as capital, with the liabilities owed to non-owners.

The 'entity view' is an extension of this, and can be contrasted to the PROPRIETARY VIEW. One view or other will be taken on major issues in accounting, like CONSOLIDATED FINANCIAL STATEMENTS and INFLATION ACCOUNTING. The entity view would see the business's viewpoint; the proprietary view sees things from the point of view of the shareholders in the parent company. Thus, in consolidation, the entity view suggests that the whole of any inter-group profit should be eliminated, even though a subsidiary was only 60 per cent owned. And, when accounting for changing prices, one would consider the effects on the assets of the business rather than on the purchasing power of the owners' capital.

Equities. – UK expression for the normal type of ownership finance, ORDINARY SHARES. It is found in a similar form in the USA as SHAREHOLDERS' EQUITY: the total of the shareholders' or stockholders' interest in a company.

Equity method. – a method used in the UK and the USA, and increasingly in other countries, as part of the preparation of CONSOLIDATED FINANCIAL STATEMENTS. It is used for those companies over which a group has 'significant influence' but not a controlling interest. A 'significant influence' is normally deemed to exist if there is a JOINT VENTURE or if between 20 and 50 per cent of the company is held. In the UK, such companies are called 'associated companies'.

The accounting treatment for such companies in consolidated financial statements is *less* than full consolidation but *more* than merely holding the investment at cost and recording dividends received. The associated company is shown in the group BALANCE SHEET at a single figure representing the fair value of its assets at the date of purchase, plus GOODWILL, plus the group's share of undistributed profits since the purchase. The first two items at the date of purchase will amount to the cost of the subsidiary. In the group PROFIT AND LOSS ACCOUNT (UK)/INCOME STATEMENT (US) the group's share of the profit of the associated company is recorded.

The rules are to be found in APB Opinion 18 and SFAS 35 in the USA, and SSAP 1 in the UK. Before these rules were made reasonably tight, practice varied, often depending upon whether the associated companies were making profits or losses! In the UK, until SSAP 1 was amended, some companies would buy or sell a few shares to arrange to be in or out of the rules in different years.

European Accounting Association. The majority of the members of this body are academic accountants from West European countries. However, there are some members from Eastern Europe, some from outside Europe, and some members are professional accountants. The main activity of the Association is its annual conference which is held in a different European city each year and is a forum for the presentation of research papers and for international discussion.

Exceptional items. – a UK expression for those items in a profit and loss account that are within the normal activities of the business, but are of unusual size. The treatment for these, as laid down in ACCOUNTING STANDARDS (SSAP 6), is to disclose them separately in the profit and loss account or the notes to it. Such items are to be distinguished from EXTRAORDINARY ITEMS.

Ex dividend. A share is 'ex div' if sales of it would not entitle the purchaser to the forthcoming dividend. So, if you buy a share in the period leading up to a dividend payment it will usually be 'ex div'. For most of the time, a share is the opposite of this, namely 'cum div'.

Expenses. When used by accountants, this is a technical term. It means all those payments, whenever physically made, that *relate* to the period in question. For example, a business may pay its electricity account after the end of the year in which the electricity was used; or it may pay its rent in advance. Such amounts are accrued expenses and prepayments, respectively. Accountants would treat both as expenses of the year to which they relate, showing the accruals or prepayments in a balance sheet.

This practice is part of the MATCHING or accruals concept. It is designed to lead to a fairer presentation of profit for a period. Profit is calculated by taking the 'expenses' from the REVENUES of the period.

A further important example of the determination of expenses relates to the purchase of fixed assets. Accountants do not charge the whole of the cost of a fixed asset against profit in the year of purchase. Instead, they charge DEPRECIATION expenses over the life of the asset; that is, they match the expenses against the periods over which the asset is contributing to profit.

Expert comptable. – nearest equivalent in France to a professionally qualified accountant in the Anglo-American sense. Most *experts comptables* are auditors of French companies. The *Ordre des Experts Comptables* is a self-regulating professional body. However, most of the rules for accounting come from government-controlled institutions, and there is also a government-controlled auditing body to which most *experts comptables* belong (see FRANCE).

Exposure drafts. – documents that precede the issue of ACCOUNTING STANDARDS. They are intended to attract response from companies, auditors, academics, investment analysts, financial institutions, etc. Frequently, responses are adverse, though contradictory when taken together. Usually, the eventual accounting standard has been adjusted in several ways before issue as a result of the comments received in the exposure period. Sometimes the comments are so strong, fundamental or numerous that a second exposure draft is issued.

Extraordinary general meeting. An EGM, as its name suggests, does not happen very often to any particular company. It will be held, within the rules laid down by company law and the company's own BYLAWS (US)/ARTICLES (UK), when certain unusual events require it. For example, a certain proportion of the shareholders may demand an EGM in order to question their directors on alleged improprieties or to deal with a takeover. An EGM may also be held when the company has solvency problems.

Normally the shareholders will only meet at the ANNUAL GENERAL MEETING.

Extraordinary items. – gains or losses which are outside the normal activities of the business, are of significant size, and are not expected to recur. An example would be the gain on the sale of a significant part of a business. The inclusion of such items would distort a view of 'sustainable' profit. On the other hand, the items did happen in the year, so there is an argument for including them. Fortunately it is possible both to include and to exclude them, by showing profits before and after extraordinary items. For the purposes of the calculation of EARNINGS PER SHARE, the extraordinary items are excluded.

The rules for extraordinary items are to be found in ACCOUNTING STANDARDS: SSAP 6 in the UK, and APB 30 in the USA. There are, however, great problems in defining exactly what an extraordinary item is. Companies can make their earnings figures better by attempting to classify as many losses (but as few gains) as possible as extraordinary. Indeed, one UK technical partner of an accounting firm has suggested that the only workable accounting standard would be for such losses to be treated as extraordinary items and such gains to be treated as EXCEPTIONAL ITEMS (the latter are included in normal profit).

F

Factoring. – an expression particularly associated with DEBTORS (UK)/ACCOUNTS RECEIVABLE (US). The 'factoring' of such debts is the selling of them to a financial institution in return for a proportion (one hopes a high proportion) of the face value. This is a technique similar to borrowing. The discount amount will be designed to include an implied rate of interest, the costs of collection and the possibility of default.

Fair presentation. Financial statements in the USA that are fully audited and prepared in accordance with GENERALLY ACCEPTED ACCOUNTING PRINCIPLES (GAAP) are required to 'fairly present' the position and results of a company. To a large extent this means obeying the rules of GAAP, but the concept of fairness transcends that, to include an assessment of the overall picture given by the financial statements. A connected doctrine is that financial statements should reflect SUBSTANCE OVER FORM.

The approximate UK equivalent is a TRUE AND FAIR VIEW.

Federation des Experts Comptables Européens. – a merger in January 1987 of the Groupe d'Etudes des Experts Comptables and the Union Européene des Experts Comptables. The FEE is a European body of accountants, one committee of which specializes in advising the EEC Commission on company law harmonization.

FIFO (first in, first out). – a common assumption for accounting purposes about the flow of items of raw materials or other INVENTORIES (stocks). It need not be expected to correspond with physical reality, but may be taken for accounting purposes. The assumption is that the first units to be received as part of inventories are the first ones to be used up or sold. This means that the most recent units are deemed to be those left at the period end. When prices are rising, and assuming a reasonably constant purchasing of materials, FIFO leads to a fairly up-to-date closing inventory figure. However, it gives an out-of-date and therefore low figure for the COST OF SALES. This leads to what many argue is an overstatement of profit figures, when prices are rising. In order to correct for this for *tax* purposes, in the UK a special STOCK RELIEF was allowed until 1984, and in the USA the use of LIFO has been allowed.

LIFO (or last in, first out) is self-explanatory. It takes the opposite assumption to FIFO, and leads to lower profits and lower balance sheet inventory figures. In the USA its use for tax purposes has to be accompanied by use in the income statement; this makes it common. In the UK, LIFO is prohibited by tax rules, and by ACCOUNTING STANDARDS (SSAP 9). In both countries, the alternative of average cost is acceptable.

Imagine the following inventory purchases and usages for FIFO, in the example on p. 80. The cost of sales would be valued at £16 (4 units at £3 and 1 unit at £4), and the inventory remaining would be valued at £20 (5 units at £4).

Using the LIFO assumption of flow, the example would lead to a charge against profit of £20 (5 units at £4) and a closing stock of £16 (1 unit at £4 and 4 units at £3). So, the charge to profit is a better estimate of current costs, but the balance sheet holds an unrealistically low stock figure.

Transaction date	Purchases	Cost of sales charged to profit	Inventory at cost
1 January	10 at £3		10 at £3 = 30
11 January		6 at £3	4 at £3 = £12
21 January	6 at £4		4 at £3 + 6 at £4 = £36
31 January		5 at ?	5 at ? = ?

Finance acts. – UK name for the annual laws that introduce tax changes and the new rates of tax. They are generally passed in the summer of each year, following Finance Bills, which themselves follow Budget Statements by the Chancellor of the Exchequer.

Financial accounting. – a fairly vague term which covers BOOKKEEPING and the subsequent processing and analysis that leads to the preparation of financial statements for shareholders and others. It may be contrasted, for example, with MANAGEMENT ACCOUNTING which deals with the use of accounting data by managers inside a business to enable better planning and control.

Financial Accounting Standards Board (FASB). – a body set up in the USA in 1973 to set ACCOUNTING STANDARDS on measurement, valuation and disclosure practices to be followed in the preparation of financial statements. In this task it is given 'substantial authoritative support' by a government body, the SECURITIES AND EXCHANGE COMMISSION (SEC). US companies that wish their securities to be publicly traded must be registered and file financial statements with the SEC, which will not accept those that disobey FASB standards. Thus the standards have considerable power, for the minority of US companies that are SEC registered.

Further, the SEC requires audits by members of the American Institute of Certified Public Accountants (AICPA) which requires its members to disclose any failure to obey standards in audit reports. The AICPA was responsible for setting accounting rules before 1973: via the ACCOUNTING PRINCIPLES BOARD from 1959 to 1973, and the Committee on Accounting Procedure before that. The rules promulgated by these three bodies constitute the bulk of GENERALLY ACCEPTED ACCOUNTING PRINCIPLES.

The FASB has seven full-time board members and a substantial research staff. The board members are appointed by the independent Financial Accounting Foundation, which also raises the money for the FASB. The donations come from companies and accounting firms, presumably fearing the intervention of the SEC if no private body were capable of setting standards. Donations are limited for any one donor, in order to preserve independence.

The FASB works by 'due process' which includes prior research, wide circulation of EXPOSURE DRAFTS, and public hearings before a standard is issued. Nevertheless many of its standards have been controversial, like those on FOREIGN CURRENCY TRANSLATION, and many have been extensively 'avoided', like that on LEASES. A major, long-running project has been the search for a CONCEPTUAL FRAMEWORK to underlie standard-setting.

The list of US standards (strictly, statements of financial accounting standards) is very long. Some of them are shown, with analogous standards of the UK, under the entry for the INTERNATIONAL ACCOUNTING STANDARDS COMMITTEE.

Financial year. – usual UK expression for the period for which the ANNUAL REPORT and accounts are prepared. The most popular dates for the year end are March 31, because this ties in best with the tax year, and December 31. Some companies account for 52 weeks, so their year end gradually changes.

In the USA, the analogous expression is FISCAL YEAR.

First-year allowance. – part of the UK's system of depreciation for tax purposes, called CAPITAL ALLOWANCES. From 1972 to 1984, investment in plant and machinery attracted a first-year allowance of 100% of the cost of the assets. This was designed to be an investment incentive. However, first-year allowances were gradually removed over a three year period from 1984 on the grounds that they introduce too much distortion into investment decisions and that, in a period of unemployment, they are not sufficiently biased in favour of job-producing projects.

Fiscal year. – US expression for the period for which companies prepare their annual financial statements. The great majority of US companies use December 31 as the fiscal year end, which corresponds with the year end for tax purposes. As an accounting term it is a slight misnomer, because 'fiscal year' really means tax year, and it is by no means for all companies that the accounting and tax years co-terminate on December 31.

In the UK, the equivalent term is FINANCIAL YEAR.

Fixed assets. – mainly a UK, rather than a US, expression, meaning the assets that are to continue to be used in the business, such as land, buildings and machines. The opposite are CURRENT ASSETS, which would be traded and expected to change their form within a year from the BALANCE SHEET date, as cash or INVENTORIES (stocks) do. The Companies Acts define fixed assets as those 'intended for use on a continuing basis'. The equivalent US expression is usually 'Property, Plant and Equipment'.

It is normal for fixed assets to wear out due to use or the effluxion of time, that is to have limited useful lives. This is recognized by a charge against profit and a reduction in the holding value of the assets, called DEPRECIATION. Some fixed assets may not wear out, such as plots of land. It may also be that the owners of Westminster Abbey, for example, might feel that its useful life is so long that depreciation is not a practical concept!

Fixed costs. – costs of a business that cannot be altered in the short term, such as factory rents or staff on contracts. For some decisions, since these costs are unalterable, they may be irrelevant. For example, when deciding what to produce in a factory next year, interest and rental costs of the factory may be irrelevant, as they will be the same whatever is decided. Further, if one is deciding when to close down a loss-making business, the alterable or variable costs may be the only relevant ones, as the fixed costs cannot be avoided whichever date is chosen.

Fixed costs will normally be OVERHEADS that relate to several product lines or jobs. For example, the chief executive's salary and the interest on loans will be fixed overhead costs.

Foreign currency translation. – the 'translation' of the financial statements of a foreign subsidiary or branch into the currency of the parent company to enable the preparation of CONSOLIDATED FINANCIAL STATEMENTS. Translation now tends to be distinguished from 'currency conversion' in that the latter involves the physical exchange of money from one currency to another. Translation is purely an accounting exercise, but a very complex and controversial one.

The 'man in the street' might think that there is little problem with currency translation. Why not use the exchange rates ruling at the balance sheet date? The problem arises because of the valuation systems used in conventional financial statements; that is, the problem stems from the use of HISTORICAL COST ACCOUNTING. For example, a French subsidiary's balance sheet may contain a plot of land 'valued' at 100,000 French francs, which is what it was bought for in 1975. When the balance sheet comes to be translated into, let us say, dollars for consolidation with its US parent's balance sheet of 1985, should the dollar/franc exchange rate of 1985 or that of 1975 be used?

The last century has seen a large number of answers to this genre of question. In the UK most companies have always used the year-end rate (the 'closing rate' or 'current rate' method). However, several methods have been used in the USA. By the mid-1960s, a method called monetary/non-monetary was in use. In this, MONETARY ASSETS and liabilities were translated at the current rate; and others at historical rates. In 1975 a theoretical basis for a similar method was outlined in an ACCOUNTING STANDARD (SFAS 8) as the 'temporal method'. In this, balances are translated at rates which relate to their valuation basis.

Mine's foreign currency. What's yours?

Thus, historic cost assets are translated at historic rates; cash is translated at the current rate; future-based receipts and payments (like accounts receivable or payable and long-term loans) are also valued at the current rate as an estimate of the future rate. This seemed like a solid piece of theory, and satisfyingly suggested that, to end up with the historic cost of a foreign asset in dollars, one had to apply the historic exchange rate to the historically valued fixed assets or inventory.

However, a severe problem arose in the late 1970s when the dollar was weak. The temporal method led to 'translation losses' in the group financial statements. This was basically because foreign fixed assets stayed at the same dollar values over time, but foreign long-term debts became worse in dollars, after translation at the current rate. This was so distasteful to large US corporations that a massive lobbying campaign against SFAS 8 was launched. This led to the introduction of the current rate method by SFAS 52 in 1981.

In the UK in 1983, a similar accounting standard to SFAS 52 was issued, i.e. SSAP 20. One of the features of the new standards was the 'net investment concept', which holds that foreign subsidiaries are usually 'separate or quasi-independent entities'. On this basis, it is argued that an across-the-board use of the closing rate is sensible, as one is not interested in the individual assets and liabilities, but in the effect on the 'net investment'. However, the problem with this argument is that the theory behind *consolidated* financial statements is that they are designed to show the parent and subsidiaries 'as if they were a single entity', thus involving the aggregation of the balance sheets, line by line. The 'theories' underlying closing rate translation and consolidation seem inconsistent.

Most of these problems would disappear if companies used some form of CURRENT VALUE ACCOUNTING. The temporal principle would then lead to the use of balance-sheet-date exchange rates for translation.

SFAS 52 calls for the use of the average-for-the-year rate for profit and loss account items. SSAP 20 allows either the average-for-the-year or the closing rate.

Practice is now fairly uniform throughout the world.

Fourth Directive. As part of the process of harmonizing the commercial rules used in the European Economic Community (Common Market), the EEC Commission drafts Directives on company law that have to be enacted in member states. The fourth Directive on company law was passed by the Council of Ministers in Brussels in 1978. It contains major provisions on accounting, and has led to new laws throughout the EEC, for example the 1981 Companies Act in the UK and similar laws in France and the Netherlands in 1983 (see DIRECTIVES OF THE EEC).

France. Financial reporting in France is quite unlike that in the UK or the USA. The reasons for this probably include the different (codified) legal system; the comparative lack of importance of private shareholders and stock exchanges as providers of finance and users of financial statements; the importance of taxation as an early use for accounting; the use of accounting by the government as an aid to the control of the economy; and the comparatively small ACCOUNTANCY PROFESSION.

French financial reporting is particularly different in its extra conservatism, its greater uniformity, its comparative lack of CONSOLI-DATED FINANCIAL STATEMENTS, its reliance on tax rules for depreciation and other valuation questions, and its greater use of provisions to enable INCOME SMOOTHING. However, as a result of EEC Directives the UK concept of the TRUE AND FAIR VIEW has now found its way into French law as the *image fidèle*, and consolidation will become standard.

The rules for French financial reporting are established by the government in detail, through several mechanisms. There are Companies Acts (notably those of 1966 and 1983), tax acts which set the level of depreciation for tax and accounting purposes, but most importantly the accounting plan (*plan comptable général*). The latter contains uniform formats for financial statements (updated in 1982 to conform with the EEC's FOURTH DIRECTIVE), uniform rules of definition and measurement, and a chart of accounts. The chart is a German invention and is now used in France to help the government to control the economy. It is a detailed decimalized system of account codes which must be filled in and returned annually by companies to the government.

The accountancy profession is small, young and weak by Anglo-Saxon comparisons. It was founded in 1942 and does not set ACCOUNT-ING STANDARDS. Power does not lie in the private body, the *Ordre des Experts Comptables*, but in the government-controlled auditing body, the *Compagnie Nationale de la Comptabilité*.

Franked investment income (FII). – dividends received by one UK company from another. These are not chargeable to CORPORATION TAX because they have already borne corporation tax in the paying company. Such income is called 'franked investment income' because it has been franked, that is taxed or stamped.

The receipt of FII by a company reduces the amount of corporation tax that has to be paid in advance as a result of its payments of dividends (see ADVANCE CORPORATION TAX).

Franked SORPs. In the UK, a 'statement of recommended practice' was a device invented in 1983 by the ACCOUNTING STANDARDS COMMITTEE

(ASC) for those rules which were thought not to be suitable for all companies or for mandatory promulgation. In some cases, it was intended that particular industries, perhaps insurance or oil, might wish to develop standardized rules for special problems and then submit them to the ASC for approval or 'franking'. The result would be a franked SORP.

Funds flow statements. – statements that are now included as a standard part of annual financial statements in the UK and, for SECURITIES AND EXCHANGE COMMISSION registered companies, in the USA. They concentrate on the changes in assets and liabilities and the causes of flows of resources into or out of a business. US and UK practices differ slightly, as does the terminology. For the US, see STATEMENTS OF CHANGES IN FINANCIAL POSITION. For the UK, see SOURCE AND APPLICATION OF FUNDS.

G

Gearing. – a measurement of the degree to which a business is funded by loans rather than SHAREHOLDERS' EQUITY. The US expression is LEVERAGE.

Different analysts of a company's financial position will use different definitions of gearing. The main rule, as with other ratios, is to try to be consistent from year to year or company to company. Common measures of gearing are long-term loans/total long-term finance, or long-term loans/shareholders' equity. The higher the proportion of loan finance, the higher is the gearing.

The origin of the use of the word gearing will become clear if we examine the effect on differently geared companies of a rise or fall in profits. For the highly geared company, increases in profits are 'geared up' for the benefit of shareholders, because the returns to the comparatively numerous lenders are fixed. For example, imagine a company with high gearing, as follows:

Share capital and reserves	300,000
Debenture loans, 10%	800,000
Net Capital employed	1,100,000

The effect of this on the rewards of the shareholders is considerable. Let us look at the profit of this company over two years. In the first year its net profit before interest and taxation is £100,000. In the second year the profit doubles to £200,000, as follows:

	Year 1	Year 2
Net profit before interest and tax	100,000	200,000
less Interest	80,000	80,000
Net profit before tax	20,000	120,000
less Taxation (at 50%, say)	10,000	60,000
Net profit after tax (earnings)	10,000	60,000

Because of the very high gearing a doubling in operating profit has led to earnings that are six times larger. In a company that can be sure of covering its heavy interest charges and expects increases in profit, the shareholders will benefit greatly from high gearing.

It is often in the best interests of the shareholders in the long run to be owners of a highly-geared company. In addition, interest costs are tax deductible, whereas dividends are not. The limit to gearing may be set by the possibility of insolvency, which may be small for a company in a low-risk line of business with rising profits, and the availability of mortgageable assets to offer to potential lenders.

A further measure of the danger of insolvency is 'interest gearing', which measures the extent to which a company's pre-tax, pre-interest profit is pre-empted by the need to pay interest. Higher interest gearing means greater danger.

Gearing adjustment. – one of the several adjustments to profit to be found in some systems of CURRENT COST ACCOUNTING that adjust profits to take account of changing prices. The main other adjustments are the DEPRECIATION and COST OF SALES ADJUSTMENT, which are extra charges against profit when prices are rising. The gearing adjustment is designed to take account of the degree to which these deductions in a particular company are compensated for by the fact that the company is financed by loans (that is, the degree to which it has high GEARING). When prices are rising, the value of loans will be declining, so that a highly geared company will be benefitting in the long run from the reduction in the real burden of its debts. The problem is that this is not a REALIZED gain until the loan is paid off. In order to avoid taking credit for unrealized gains, which would be seen by accountants as against normal CONSERVATISM, the gearing adjustment adds back a proportion of the other current cost adjustments. The gearing proportion is approximately the long-term *loan* finance divided by the total long-term finance.

Gearing adjustments, particularly that in SSAP 16 in the UK, have been heavily criticized as lacking in logic and as merely excuses for making profits look larger. The SSAP 16 gearing adjustment has even been accused (with some justification) of being invented by economists; a serious handicap for any accounting practice!

Generally accepted accounting principles (GAAP). – a technical term, particularly used in the USA, to include the ACCOUNTING STANDARDS of the FINANCIAL ACCOUNTING STANDARDS BOARD, and extant rules of predecessor bodies (for example Accounting Research Bulletins and APB Opinions). Also included are some of the rules propounded by the SECURITIES AND EXCHANGE COMMISSION (SEC) as Accounting Series Releases.

The SEC requires that companies registered with it prepare audited financial statements according to US GAAP.

Generally accepted auditing standards (GAAS). – a technical term, used in the USA, to include those rules that should be followed by auditors when carrying out a 'full' audit on financial statements, particularly for SECURITIES AND EXCHANGE COMMISSION filing purposes.

GAAS includes ethical rules of the AMERICAN INSTITUTE OF CERTIFIED

PUBLIC ACCOUNTANTS; rules on the independence of auditors from clients; and rules on the type and amount of work to be done.

General purchasing power accounting (GPP). – a term used to describe several similar systems of adjustment to HISTORICAL COST ACCOUNTING to take account of the effects of inflation. These systems only affect accounting when the annual (or more frequent) financial statements are prepared. They comprise a series of adjustments to the historical cost figures. Roughly, all the figures in the financial statements are increased by the change in inflation (usually a government prices index is used).

Fixed assets and stocks are presented at amounts indexed up to the balance sheet date from their purchase date. Monetary assets and liabilities are left at their face values. Most revenues and expenses are already expressed in current terms (at least, for the accounting period, if not the year end). However, adjustments are necessary for DE-PRECIATION and COST OF SALES. Also, in the calculation of profit, a gain or loss on monetary items is usually included.

In the UK, such systems are usually known as CURRENT PURCHASING POWER ACCOUNTING (CPP). In 1974, the UK accountancy profession favoured the adoption of CPP, but was effectively overruled by a government report of 1975, the Sandilands Report. This has been followed by a decade of controversy about which method of CURRENT COST ACCOUNTING to adopt.

In the USA, the equivalent system, General Price Level Adjusted Accounting was also favoured by the profession in the early 1970s, but not by the SEC. The ACCOUNTING STANDARD, SFAS 33, originally required large companies to disclose supplementary information on both a GPP 'constant dollar' basis and a replacement cost basis.

In countries with very high inflation, like many South American countries, GPP has been adopted for accounting. This is partly because there is no sufficiently large or skilled body of accountants to operate a more complicated specific-price-change accounting system.

Germany. Financial reporting in West Germany is very substantially different from that in the UK or the USA. See the entry for WEST GERMANY.

Gilt-edged securities. – UK expression for some loans made to the government. So secure are the interest payments and eventual repayment deemed to be, that this form of loan stock is seen to be almost risk-free or 'as good as gold', hence 'gilt-edged'. Another name for certain types of government securities is 'Treasury bills'. This opens the door to the possibility of extreme confusion for UK accountants and businessmen when they meet the expression TREASURY STOCK in US balance sheets. In the USA, 'treasury stock' means a company's own shares bought back by the company and held in the corporate treasury. The UK expression for this is OWN SHARES.

GmbH. – abbreviation for a German or Swiss private limited company, a *Gesellschaft mit beschränkter Haftung*. It is not the exact equivalent of a UK private company or a US non-registered company; but is a little like a partnership in its ownership stock. There are about 200,000 GmbHs in West Germany. They are subject to the accounting and company law rules of the GmbH-Gesetz. Before the implementation of the EEC's FOURTH DIRECTIVE, all except the very largest GmbHs did not have to be audited or to publish accounts. Now these exemptions are restricted to a much smaller number of smaller GmbHs.

Going concern. – an important underlying concept in accounting practice. The assumption for most businesses is that they will continue for the foreseeable future. This means that, for most purposes, the break-up or forced-sale value of the assets is not relevant. Particularly for fixed assets, what they could be sold for may be a severe underestimate of their value to a business in terms of REPLACEMENT COST or ECONOMIC VALUE. Thus, their NET REALIZABLE VALUE is ignored in most systems of accounting, including the conventional system, HISTORICAL COST ACCOUNTING.

Companies do not need to disclose that they are following the going concern convention. However, if there are doubts that a business is a going concern, the convention should be abandoned in order to show realizable values where appropriate. The company should do this and disclose it but, if they do not, the auditors must make plain reference to the problem in their report, with a 'going concern qualification'.

Goodwill. – the amount paid for a business in excess of the fair value of its assets at the date of acquisition. It exists because a GOING CONCERN business is usually worth more than the sum of the values of its separable NET ASSETS. This may be looked upon as its ability to earn future profits above those of a similar newly formed company, or it may be seen as the 'goodwill' of customers, the established network of contacts, loyal staff and skilled management.

If the business being bought is unincorporated (like a partnership) it will be absorbed into the legal and accounting entity of the acquiring company. Any resulting goodwill, shown in the BALANCE SHEET of the company, might be called 'purchased goodwill'. In the more usual cases, where a *company* is bought, the resulting goodwill in the CONSOLIDATED FINANCIAL STATEMENTS is called 'goodwill on consolidation'.

Assets are brought into the consolidated financial statements at their fair value rather than their BOOK VALUE because the former is a better indication of the 'cost' to the group of companies of the newly arrived assets. The exception to this practice is POOLING OF INTERESTS (US)/MERGER ACCOUNTING (UK).

The US treatment for goodwill is to show it in the balance sheet and to write it off gradually against profit in annual instalments of DEPRECIATION, over a period not exceeding 40 years. (The rules are in APB Opinion 17.) In the UK, normal practice (SSAP 22) is to treat goodwill as an asset but to write it off against group RESERVES immediately on acquisition. This is convenient, as it avoids showing a rather shadowy asset and it avoids reducing reported profits as a result of depreciation charges. However, in neither country is it now acceptable to show goodwill as an asset without depreciating it. This is gradually becoming established in law (UK) and ACCOUNTING STANDARDS (UK and USA) because it is argued that the goodwill which was acquired at the date of acquisition wears out, even though it will probably be replaced by new goodwill due to spending money on training, recruitment, advertising, etc.

Thus, the 'goodwill' shown in a balance sheet should not normally be taken as a reasonable estimate of the value of a business above its tangible net assets. That goodwill will be out-of-date, depreciated and, possibly, fully written off.

Governmental Accounting Standards Board (GASB). – US standard-setting body that represents a recent extension of the work of the Financial Accounting Foundation which also controls the FINANCIAL ACCOUNTING STANDARDS BOARD. GASB's task is to develop accounting standards for government-controlled enterprises.

Gross profit. – for a UK manufacturing company, the difference between the value of its sales and the COST OF SALES. The latter includes the purchases of raw materials, adjusted for changes to stocks (INVENTORIES), and all the other costs of producing the goods that were sold in the period, such as factory wages. From the gross profit, one would then deduct non-manufacturing expenses, like administration costs and interest charges, to arrive at net profit before tax.

Two outline formats for the profit and loss account are allowed by the COMPANIES ACTS; Format 1 involves the calculation of gross profit, which may thus be seen in the published financial statements of some companies.

The gross profit on each unit of production may be called the 'gross margin'.

Group accounts. – UK expression to describe the financial statements of a group of companies (the parent company and its subsidiaries). The COMPANIES ACTS require group accounts to be prepared by groups, and this normally means CONSOLIDATED FINANCIAL STATEMENTS.

Groupe d'Etudes des Experts Comptables de la CEE. The EEC Accountants' Study Group was set up at the request of the Commission of the European Communities. Its task was to respond to the Commission on matters concerning accountants, particularly draft DIRECTIVES. Its functions have been absorbed into the FEDERATION DES EXPERTS COMPTABLES EUROPEENS.

H

Harmonization. – the making of practices more compatible, though not necessarily exactly standardized. The word is commonly used in the context of the effort of the Commission of the European Communities to bring about compatibility of financial reporting and company law in the Common Market. Of course, what is necessary for this is *enforceability*. This is achieved by passing DIRECTIVES on company law (see that entry for a list), which have to be enacted and enforced by member states.

There is a long way to go, but here are some examples of significant progress so far:

1   The UK and the Netherlands have now followed other EEC countries by adopting uniform formats for financial statements, which are not only approximately standardized within a country, but are broadly comparable throughout the EEC.

2   France and West Germany are adopting the overriding convention of the TRUE AND FAIR VIEW, and financial statements must disclose the effect of tax-based rules.

3   Anglo-Dutch concepts of the need for CONSOLIDATED FINANCIAL STATEMENTS are being adopted throughout the EEC, which is a major change for most member states.

4   The need for audit and publication of financial statements for most private companies is being adopted throughout the EEC, as already practised in the UK and Ireland.

Historical cost accounting. – the conventional system of accounting, widely established throughout the world, except in some countries where inflation is endemic and high, and even there the GENERAL PURCHASING POWER ACCOUNTING system is a set of simple adjustments carried out annually from historical cost records.

Under historical cost accounting, the purchases of assets, such as land, buildings, machines and inventories (stocks), are recorded at their purchase price at the date of acquisition. Generally that value is not subsequently changed except to write down the value below cost in order to recognize any loss in value or normal wearing out. The latter is known as DEPRECIATION. Other balances, like DEBTORS (UK)/ACCOUNTS RECEIVABLE (US) or various sorts of liabilities are valued at what is expected to be received or paid in cash. This is the case under historical cost and most other systems.

Historical cost has a number of advantages, which explain its continued dominance. First, the original purpose of accounting was accountability or STEWARDSHIP; that is, it was designed to enable the owners of resources (such as shareholders) to check up on their managers or stewards (such as company directors). For this purpose, there is an advantage in reporting what was spent by the directors to buy assets. Any revaluations would obscure the actions of the directors. Also, accountability suggests the need for OBJECTIVITY of measurement and for ease of audit. Historical cost involves less estimation than alternatives such as REPLACEMENT COST, NET REALIZABLE VALUE or ECONOMIC VALUE. Furthermore, it is cheap to use because its values are already recorded and it requires no complex annual adjustments.

Can there, then, be anything wrong with this well-tried, objective and cheap system? Well, yes, there can. Historical cost has been accused of producing figures that are totally irrelevant! Why might one wish to know the historical cost of a piece of land bought in 1948? Worse, why might one wish to know the total of the cost of two pieces of land: one bought in 1948 and another in 1975? In times of inflation, the out-of-date values involved and the addition of prices of different periods leads to figures that are hard to interpret; and it is very difficult to see how one could use them for any decision-making purpose.

In recent decades, financial reporting has been seen increasingly as an aid to decision-making. Shareholders will want to know whether to buy, hold or sell shares in a particular company. Lenders will have similar decisions to make. Managers will want to know whether to sell their company's assets and whether to expand or contract. Historical costs are not good measures for these decisions.

Historical cost profit measurements are just as deficient as its valuations. Historical cost depreciation charges are proportions of out-of-date costs; and historical cost of sales is also based on out-of-date inventory prices (see COST OF SALES ADJUSTMENT). Thus, when prices are rising, historical cost accounting overstates the size of operating profits by including HOLDING GAINS or 'cost savings'. This may lead to incorrect decisions on dividends, wages, prices and production plans.

As a result of these problems, various systems of INFLATION ACCOUNTING have been proposed from the late 1960s onwards. However, because of the complexities, costs and other disadvantages of all its competitors, historical cost is still the dominant system. Nevertheless, in the Netherlands, some companies have prepared replacement cost financial statements since the 1950s. Also, in most English-speaking countries, supplementary information based on replacement costs has been produced as part of the financial reporting of large companies.

Holding company. – a company that owns or controls others. In the narrow use of the expression, it implies that the company does not actively trade but operates through various subsidiaries. The accounting treatment for such parent-subsidiary relationships is to prepare CONSOLIDATED FINANCIAL STATEMENTS for the combined group.

Holding gains. During periods of rising prices, the NET REALIZABLE VALUE of some fixed assets and inventories (stocks) will rise. When these assets are sold, perhaps as buildings to be replaced or as finished goods, the gain realized is not due to the normal trading operations of the business but is a 'holding gain'. In the case of assets that are consumed in order to make profit, like plant, it may be said that there are 'cost savings' as a result of having bought the plant for less than the current price.

Holding gains may, of course, also be realiz*able*, up to the point of sale of the asset concerned. Conventional HISTORICAL COST ACCOUNTING ignores realizable holding gains, and records only the realized gains. Thus, profits are distorted, particularly in the year of sale of significant assets. Most systems of INFLATION ACCOUNTING either deduct or separately identify some version of holding gains, in order to calculate 'operating profit'.

A simple example relating to holding gains on inventories may be found under the entry for COST OF SALES ADJUSTMENT.

Human assets. It is clear that the total value of some businesses rests heavily on their human assets, like loyal staff and skilled and trained managers. At the extreme, the value of 'owning' a football or basketball team may rest almost entirely on human assets. In conventional accounting, such assets have been ignored because of the difficulty of establishing an objective and auditable value. The future ECONOMIC VALUE of employees is obviously hard to determine with any accuracy and, even if one were to use HISTORICAL COST ACCOUNTING, it would not be clear exactly what was spent on creating the assets, nor how much of what was spent was wasted.

Nevertheless, some schemes for the valuation of human assets have been worked out. They involve the accumulation of such costs as recruitment and training, with a reduction for staff who have left. Practical application has not followed these theoretical exercises; so human assets remain a part of the mysterious total of GOODWILL.

Hyde Guidelines. As part of the long-running saga of the development of a system of INFLATION ACCOUNTING in the UK, some 'interim guidelines' were developed in 1977 by a sub-committee of the ACCOUNTING STANDARDS COMMITTEE chaired by William Hyde, Treasurer of the University of Oxford. These guidelines were a rapid response to the rejection of the proposals for CURRENT COST ACCOUNTING (CCA) of ED 18 by the membership of the Institute of Chartered Accountants in England and Wales.

The Guidelines called for large companies to prepare supplementary

profit and loss accounts on a CCA basis, including a GEARING ADJUST-
MENT. They were followed by fuller proposals in ED 24, and then by
the accounting standard on CCA, SSAP 16, in 1980.

I

Income. The words 'REVENUES', 'PROFIT', 'EARNINGS' and 'income' are used somewhat vaguely by some accountants and businessmen, and usage in the UK and the USA is slightly different.

In the UK, 'income' tends not to be used in connection with commercial businesses. Instead, there are sales revenues, gross and net profits and earnings (in increasing order of the extraction of expenses). The word 'income' is associated more with NOT-FOR-PROFIT organizations.

In the USA, 'income' tends to be used more widely in a commercial context, instead of 'profit'.

Income and expenditure account. – a version of the PROFIT AND LOSS ACCOUNT for NOT-FOR-PROFIT organizations. It retains the MATCHING concept that concentrates on revenues and expenses of a period. The alternative, RECEIPTS AND PAYMENTS ACCOUNT, concentrates on cash movements instead.

Thus, the income and expenditure account for a period shows the revenues and expenses relating to that period, and concludes with a calculation of the surplus or deficit for the period.

Income smoothing. – reducing the variation in yearly profit figures. In some countries the main providers of finance are generally very long-run investors like founding families or governments or bankers (acting as owners as well as lenders). In such cases, actively trading private or institutional shareholders may be unimportant compared to their position in the English-speaking world (see LISTED COMPANIES). Countries where outside shareholders are less important include FRANCE and WEST GERMANY. In these cases, there is less need for published financial statements, for audit and for a FAIR PRESENTATION of a particular year's results. Instead, the long-run owners may prefer a long-run picture of progress, which will involve the smoothing out of yearly variations in profit. This can be done by charging high PROVISIONS for depreciation, risks or contingencies in successful years, and by charging lower depreciation or by reducing contingency provisions in poor years. In some countries these provision 'slush funds' can be enormous, and can enable such lavish smoothing that the real results of individual years are quite hidden in the final 'profit' announcements. Thus, someone used to ANGLO-SAXON ACCOUNTING should take care in reading the financial statements of countries using quite different systems.

Income statement. – the usual US name for the statement of revenues and expenses of a particular period, leading to the calculation of net income or net profit. For companies registered with the SECURITIES AND EXCHANGE COMMISSION a full annual income statement must be published, and quarterly and half-yearly information must also be published. The income statement shows the annual sales and other revenues, and then the expenses or costs of manufacture, administration, marketing, interest and taxation.

The format of the income statement is usually 'vertical' or 'statement' form rather than 'horizontal', 'two-sided' or 'account' form.

The equivalent UK statement is the PROFIT AND LOSS ACCOUNT. The complement to the income statement is the BALANCE SHEET which shows the assets and liabilities of the business at a point in time. The balance sheet deals with the inventory of assets and liabilities at the balance sheet date; the income statement deals with *flows* of revenues and expenses over a *period*.

Income tax. All forms of businesses in the USA pay income tax. In the UK, unincorporated businesses pay income tax, but companies pay corporation tax.

Income tax is calculated by applying a series of stepped, increasing marginal rates to taxable income, which is based on the net profit for accounting purposes but with some adjustments, notably in the UK (where the rules are similar to those for CORPORATION TAX).

In the USA, income tax is paid on a quarterly prepayment system, using estimates based on the previous year's profits. A major adjustment is the INVESTMENT TAX CREDIT which is an investment incentive. This involves the reduction of tax liabilities by an amount based on a pro-

'Remind me once more of the amazing tax advantages'

portion of amounts spent on property, plant and equipment purchases. A further adjustment is partially to exempt receipts of dividends from subsidiary or other related companies.

As a result of some timing differences between when expenses are taken for accounting purposes and allowed for tax purposes, DEFERRED TAX may arise.

Incomplete records. – partial accounting records. The full DOUBLE ENTRY bookkeeping system is exceptionally useful for the recording of transactions and the running of a business. However, it is somewhat complex, time-consuming and expensive. Consequently, some businesses that are small or badly organized do not keep what might be called 'proper books of account'. Instead, there may be a cash book, a list of sales, and records on the backs of envelopes. This can be described by the broad term 'incomplete records'. Of course the problem will also occur if the books are mislaid, stolen or burnt.

Accountants are quite good at taking incomplete records and reconstructing what must have happened, with the aid of bank statements, last year's BALANCE SHEET, and so on. This is necessary to calculate profits for the information of the owner and the tax authorities.

Indirect costs. – costs of a business that cannot be directly associated with the production of a particular unit or type of product. Examples are: machines used for the production of a variety of products at different times of the day; the supervising staff in a factory who look after several product lines; and the heating and rental costs of a manufacturing unit that produces several products.

The problem is that, if you need to calculate the full cost of production of particular units, some arbitrary 'allocation' of these costs must be made to the various units or products. Such 'full costing' or 'absorption costing' (which absorbs all the overheads) may be thought useful for production decisions, for setting prices and for calculating detailed profitability. However, the results may be misleading, since other allocations would have been possible. Also, although some overheads are variable, others are 'fixed' in the short run, so that dropping a particular product will not reduce such costs at all.

Inflation accounting. – usually interpreted as encompassing all sorts of systems that might adjust or replace HISTORICAL COST ACCOUNTING to take account of changing prices. Many such systems are poorly described by the term, because they do not involve a recognition of general price level movements. Systems that do adjust for *inflation* are called GENERAL PURCHASING POWER ACCOUNTING (GPP), CURRENT PURCHAS-

ING POWER ACCOUNTING (UK), general price level adjusted accounting (USA) or constant dollar accounting (USA).

Alternatives that adjust for the specific price changes affecting the assets and operations of a business are CURRENT COST ACCOUNTING, REPLACEMENT COST ACCOUNTING, and systems that rely on NET REALIZABLE VALUES and ECONOMIC VALUES.

In nearly all systems of 'inflation accounting' there are adjustments of balance sheet assets each year, and also adjustments to profit for DEPRECIATION and COST OF SALES. In some systems there are also adjustments for monetary items, including a GEARING ADJUSTMENT.

In practice, most countries have remained faithful to historical cost for the main financial statements of businesses. However, in some South American countries with very high rates of inflation, GPP has been adopted. In the Netherlands, some companies use replacement cost accounting, and others provide notes on this basis. In the English-speaking world, large companies provide supplementary price-adjusted data. For more detail, see CURRENT COST ACCOUNTING and CAPITAL MAINTENANCE CONCEPT.

'Here's how it works − they base their pay claim on our historic cost accounting profits and we base our offer on inflation adjusted profits'

Initial allowance. – part of the UK CAPITAL ALLOWANCES system of depreciation for tax purposes. However, in the mid-1980s, capital allowances have been greatly simplified, so that 'initial allowance' is no longer an important expression.

Insider dealing. – the use of information, that is not publicly available, to make decisions about buying or selling publicly traded shares. For example, company executives and auditors may know about unexpected profits well before a public announcement of them. By buying shares themselves or by giving the information to friends or relatives, profits may be made.

Insider dealing is now illegal in the UK; and this involves a number of complex definitions of associated persons.

Insolvency. – a state in which a business or person is unable to pay debts as they fall due. Expertise in dealing with insolvency and BANKRUPTCY was fundamental to the emergence of the accountancy profession in the UK in the second half of the nineteenth century.

Institutes of accountants. The earliest professional bodies of accountants were those formed in Edinburgh and Glasgow in the 1850s. Later, England and then the USA followed with Institutes of 'Chartered' or 'Certified Public' accountants. Similar bodies were formed throughout the English-speaking world in the late nineteenth century. Initially, members concentrated on INSOLVENCY and BANKRUPTCY, but later the emphasis moved to AUDITING. More details of the bodies and their work may be found in the entry for ACCOUNTANCY PROFESSION.

Insurance company. For the purposes of company law or, in the case of the USA, the SECURITIES AND EXCHANGE COMMISSION, the concept of 'insurance company' is closely defined. Such companies have different accounting and reporting requirements from those of normal commercial enterprises. In the USA, an accounting standard (SFAS 60) deals with insurance company accounting.

Intangible assets. – assets that are not physical or tangible. As explained under the heading ASSET, accountants use a variety of (what some might call peculiar) rules in order to decide, first, whether to treat an item as an asset and, second, how to value it. The greatest problems of this sort relate to intangible assets, as opposed to tangible assets like property, plant and equipment. Intangible assets that may be shown on a balance sheet include patents, trade marks and GOODWILL. However, in the case of goodwill, it is standard practice to include only those assets which have been bought by the business, not those created by it. This is because only those bought from outsiders will have a reliable 'cost'; the objectivity of HISTORICAL COST ACCOUNTING is fundamental to conventional financial reporting. It is at cost, less any diminution in value, that the intangibles will be shown. Intangibles are reduced in value by DEPRECIATION over their useful lives.

In the UK, it is normal not to show goodwill in balance sheets and to depreciate it, but to write it off immediately against reserves. Also, unlike US practice, it is acceptable to treat some applied DEVELOPMENT EXPENDITURE as an asset and, later, to treat it as expenses when the expected profits are made.

Interest. – the payment made to lenders. It may be contrasted to the payments to shareholders, who receive DIVIDENDS. Interest is a compulsory payment, so an unpaid lender can take legal action against the defaulting company. Interest is paid at a fixed rate. It is part of the EXPENSES of a business, and is tax deductible for the purposes of income tax (US)/corporation tax (UK).

Interim reports and dividends. 'Interim report' is the UK expression for a half-yearly report for companies listed on the Stock Exchange. Such reports must be published, but they are not audited and are not very detailed compared to an ANNUAL REPORT. These reports are required in order to inform shareholders and to allow share prices to adjust during the year rather than waiting for the annual profit announcement.

Also, it is normal for large UK companies to declare an 'interim dividend' which may be about one third of the expected dividend for the full year.

In the USA, quarterly interim reports are required from companies registered with the SECURITIES AND EXCHANGE COMMISSION. Also, quarterly dividends are common.

Internal audit. – the examination of the systems of control and the accuracy of records of a company by its own staff. This may be distinguished from external AUDITING which involves the checking, *by or for* the owners of resources or companies, *on* the stewards or managers of those resources. This is called 'external audit', because it is done for those who are not day-to-day managers, and it is now usually done by independent professional experts.

In addition to this ancient activity of external audit, managers of companies in recent years have devoted more and more energy to 'internal audit'. To some extent this duplicates or pre-empts the work of external auditors, and may reduce the work and fees of the latter. However, internal audit tends also to be actively concerned with the discovery and prevention of fraud and with the installation and smooth running of efficient systems of control. These latter are not the main concerns of external auditors, who are appointed to give their opinion on the fairness of the financial statements.

Internal check. – one part of INTERNAL CONTROL: office systems designed to make error and fraud difficult. Internal check rests on the separation of duties achieved when two or more employees are involved in control processes. At its simplest, this suggests that at least two people should have to sign or be involved in the completion of cheques or the distribution of cash wages. Good internal check also involves the rotation of duties and insistence on holidays for employees. This ensures that certain elaborate frauds involving the falsification of records cannot be covered up indefinitely.

Internal control. – all those management systems controlling the administration of an organization. This will include INTERNAL AUDIT, INTERNAL CHECK and BUDGETS. Good internal control will make error and fraud more difficult, and will also make accounting records more reliable. Less detailed AUDITING of individual documents and transactions will be necessary if the internal control is good.

Internal rate of return (IRR). The IRR of a project or a proposed project is the annual percentage profitability on the initial investment, taking into account the fact that money received later is worth less than money received earlier. The rate calculated can be compared to the assumed interest cost for the capital used in the project. The interest cost will depend upon the company's individual sources and uses of finance. Projects with higher internal rates of return will be preferred to those with lower; and all projects carried out should have internal rates of return that exceed the cost of the capital.

The NET PRESENT VALUE method involves similar calculations but is regarded as a more reliable means of discriminating between projects.

International Accounting Standards Committee (IASC). – an organization composed of representatives of over 70 professional accountancy bodies from different countries. It was formed in 1973 and has its headquarters in London. Its purpose is to devise and promulgate international standards in order to reduce the variation of practices in financial reporting throughout the world. Its member bodies have promised to use their best endeavours to ensure compliance with standards. The standards are generally compromises between US and UK practices.

A sample of IASC Standards is listed below, with UK and US equivalents. By 1986, 26 Standards had been issued.

	IASC	UK	USA
Disclosure of Accounting Policies	IAS 1	SSAP 2	APB 20 APB 22
Valuation and Presentation of Inventories	IAS 2 IAS 11	SSAP 9	ARB 43 ARB 45
Consolidated Financial Statements	IAS 3	SSAP 1 SSAP 14	ARB 43, 51 APB 16, 17
Depreciation Accounting	IAS 4	SSAP 12 SSAP 19	ARB 43 APB 12
Statement of Changes in Financial Position	IAS 7	SSAP 10	(SEC, S-X) APB 19
Unusual and Prior Period Items	IAS 8	SSAP 6	APB 16, 30 SFAS 4, 16
Accounting for R and D	IAS 9	SSAP 13	SFAS 2
Contingencies and Post Balance Sheet Events	IAS 10	SSAP 17 SSAP 18	SFAS 5

International Federation of Accountants (IFAC). – a body comprising representatives from the accountancy professions of many nations. It was formed in 1977, and is based in New York. Its largest task is the organization of the four-yearly World Congresses of Accountants. It also has committees that try to promote international harmonization of auditing and management accounting. However, it leaves the area of accounting standards to the IASC (see preceding entry).

Inventories. – raw materials, work-in-progress and goods ready for sale. In the UK, the word 'stocks' is generally used instead.

The valuation of inventories is a very important exercise for a business. The figure usually forms an important part of the CURRENT ASSETS total on a balance sheet, and it is a vital part of the calculation of profit. The GROSS PROFIT of a business is the sales *less* the cost of sales. The cost of sales is the purchases of goods, adjusted for the change in the level of inventories during the period, plus certain costs (see below).

Before inventories can be valued, they must be counted. Some businesses run a 'continuous (or perpetual) inventory', an elaborate recording system supplemented by occasional physical counts of particular inventories in order to check the records. In other businesses, an annual physical inventory count (or, in the UK, a 'stock take') is performed, sometimes involving the closing of the business for one day at the year end. Normally, because the value of inventories is so important, the auditors of a business will attend the count and will make careful checks on all aspects of it.

Having counted the inventory, the next stage is to value it. The normal valuation method is to use 'the lower of cost and market value'. The use of cost is a normal method of accounting for all assets, under the HISTORICAL COST ACCOUNTING convention. However, because inventories are current assets and may soon be sold, their market value will also be relevant. The principle of CONSERVATISM causes accountants to reduce the value of inventories below cost in those, fairly unusual cases, where market value has fallen below cost. 'Market value' in the UK means NET REALIZABLE VALUE, although in the USA it can mean CURRENT REPLACEMENT COST where this is lower.

'Cost' includes all the expenses associated with the purchase of inventories, plus those costs of bringing them to their existing condition and location, this includes production overheads. For most inventories, it is either impossible or impracticable to know the precise units of raw material, etc that are being used up in production or that remain at the year end. Thus, it is normal for accountants to make assumptions about the flow of such inventories. Such assumptions include: first in, first out (FIFO); last in, first out (LIFO); and average cost (AVCO). In the UK, FIFO and AVCO are normal, whereas LIFO is not allowed for taxation purposes and is discouraged by the relevant ACCOUNTING STANDARD (SSAP 9). In the USA, LIFO is allowed for tax purposes. It usually reduces income, so it is popular – more details are given under the entries for FIFO and LIFO.

One further problem for inventory valuation is what to do about long-term contracts. For these, there may be work-in-progress for several years before a project is finally completed. It is normal practice to take a proportion of profit as production proceeds, assuming that there is an agreed sale and an expected eventual profit.

Investment properties. – properties held by a business for investment potential or rental income, rather than for owner occupation. Thus, investment properties may be owned by businesses other than investment companies.

In the UK, property companies have always been opposed to the charging of depreciation on investment properties, claiming that such charges are unrealistic. They persuaded the ACCOUNTING STANDARDS COMMITTEE to exempt them from the depreciation standard (SSAP 12). Subsequently, the 1981 Companies Act required all fixed assets with limited useful lives to be depreciated. However, an accounting standard especially for investment properties (SSAP 19) was produced; this required annual revaluation but no depreciation.

The apparent inconsistency between the accounting standard and the Companies Acts should be explained here. The overriding requirement of the Companies Acts is that financial statements should give a TRUE AND FAIR VIEW. The accounting standard (SSAP 19) developed an 'argument' against depreciation and then claimed that the practices prescribed by the standard were designed to give a true and fair view. Thus, lack of depreciation of investment properties appears to become suitable, despite one of the detailed requirements of law. There is some disquiet in legal, governmental and accounting circles about this rather cavalier approach to the law.

Investment tax credit. – a US tax incentive for companies who purchased property, plant and equipment. The tax credit was equivalent to ten per cent of the purchase price. It was repealed for January 1987 onwards.

There were two main accounting treatments for the tax credit: allocating it over the life of the asset, and taking benefit in the income statement immediately. The former treatment was proposed by the ACCOUNTING PRINCIPLES BOARD in 1962. However, this made the tax credit less noticeable in the income statement. As a result of this, in a rare intervention, Congress stated in 1971 that no body could make an authoritative rule on the appropriate accounting treatment. Consequently, most US companies took benefit immediately; this was called the 'flow through' method.

Investment trusts. – companies whose main purpose is to use the funds contributed by shareholders to own and manage profitably a portfolio of stocks and shares. Unlike UNIT TRUSTS, these are 'closed-ended funds' in that there are no extra regular contributions from participants. If a shareholder wishes to extract his funds, he must sell his shares to another investor. This would have no direct effect on the trust.

Irredeemable debenture. Securities are 'irredeemable' if there is no provision for their holders to be paid back by the issuing company. Normally, loans are redeemable but shares are not. However, there are exceptions to both these rules; and in the UK there are loans called 'irredeemable DEBENTURES'.

Of course, even where securities are irredeemable, there is normally a market in them. Irredeemable debentures are valuable because of the future flows of interest coming from them. Thus, their value at any moment depends on this flow, and on the market rate of interest at that moment. As the market rate rises, so the value of any particular debenture falls, because its future interest rate is fixed.

Issued share capital. – the amount of share capital of a company, at PAR VALUE, that has been subscribed by shareholders. The MEMORANDUM (UK)/CERTIFICATE OF INCORPORATION (US) of a company details the maximum share capital that is authorized for a company, although this can be changed by the shareholders. Often, a company will not have issued as many shares as are authorized. The issued capital will be shown in the BALANCE SHEET, and the authorized share capital will be shown in the notes to the financial statements.

All shares in the UK, and most shares in the USA, have a nominal or par value. This is little more than a label for a particular type of share. Normally, shares will be sold by a company at a price above the par value. In the financial statements, such shares are recorded 'at par' under the heading of share capital, common stock (US), etc. The excess contributed above the par value is shown as SHARE PREMIUM (UK) or capital surplus/PAID-IN SURPLUS (US).

J

Japan. Japanese accounting is a mixture of mediaeval Japanese book-keeping, overlaid by German company law imported in the late nineteenth century, plus American style rules concerning the accountancy profession, the stock exchange and disclosure requirements. The American influence came in the late 1940s onwards.

Thus, there is a dominance of loan finance and of tax-based accounting, as in WEST GERMANY.

Joint venture. – a co-operative exercise between two or more businesses, usually set up for a specific purpose and a limited time. In the mediaeval world, joint ventures became common as a means of funding large projects, like commercial voyages to the East. More recently, joint ventures have begun to operate in the North Sea, prospecting for oil. They are a means of temporarily pooling resources and skills.

In some countries there are standard legal formats for this purpose; for example, the *groupement d'intérêt économique* in France. The latter form was copied in 1985 by the EEC for a multinational joint venture format: the European Economic Interest Grouping.

Journal entries. In many businesses there are, quite literally, millions of transactions each day. The DOUBLE ENTRY system has to record all these. However, there is a danger that the main BOOKS of account will get swamped with information. Thus, for some very frequent events, like sales, there are special DAY BOOKS. The 'journal', as its name suggests, is also a day book; it contains a record of the creation of double entries for those types of item that are not sufficiently frequent to have their own specialized day book, such as year-end entries and the correction of errors. Every DEBIT or CREDIT that is recorded will have gone through a day book. Thus, all entries can be traced back to their source, where a description and date can be found.

L

Leases. Leasing can take several forms: one can lease a used car for three months, lease a new machine for all of its useful life, or lease an apartment for sixty years. In the last case, it would be normal to purchase the lease; whereas, for machines or cars, it would be normal to make period payments throughout the agreed term of the lease.

A lease agreement on machines or cars commits the lessee to fixed future payments for a certain length of time, in return for the legal right to use the leased asset. However, the asset is still the legal property of the lessor, and it reverts to him at the end of the lease.

For leases of new plant that are expected to last for most of the useful life of the asset, the act of leasing is very similar to hire purchase, or to a purchase plus a loan from the lessor. In the last two cases, accountants would treat the plant as an asset and would record the future liabilities. In recent years, it has become standard practice to do this for leased assets also. This is despite the fact that the assets are not owned by the lessee. It is considered that the capitalized leases exhibit a fair view, and represent SUBSTANCE OVER FORM.

The rules may be found in SFAS 13 in the USA, and in SSAP 21 in the UK. Because the capitalization of leases adds significantly to the recorded assets and liabilities of the business, it makes LIQUIDITY, PROFITABILITY and LEVERAGE/GEARING look worse. Thus, it is unpopular with some companies, and there have been many examples of 'avoidance' by finding loopholes in the rules.

Ledgers. – another name for some of the BOOKS of account of a business. The 'sales ledger' contains lists of amounts due from customers; there will also be a purchases ledger. These are 'personal ledgers', in that they deal with debts to and from persons. There are also 'real ledgers' that deal with property, plant and equipment; and 'nominal ledgers' that deal with ACCOUNTS that are not real or personal, for example interest costs or depreciation charges. However, the above three categories tend now not to be differentiated; the whole set tend to be called 'the nominal ledger'. In many businesses, there are no longer books or ledgers, but computer tapes.

Leverage. – US term for the degree to which a business is funded by loans rather than by shareholders' equity. In a highly levered company, a percentage increase in trading profit will be magnified by the time it reaches the shareholders, because the return to the lenders is a fixed amount of interest. This is illustrated under the entry for GEARING, which is the equivalent UK expression.

Liabilities. – amounts of money that must be paid by a business at some future date. Most liabilities are of known amount and date. They include long-term loans, bank overdrafts and amounts owed to suppliers. There are current and non-current liabilities. The former are expected to be paid within a year from the date of the BALANCE SHEET on which they appear. The calculation of LIQUIDITY includes knowing the total of current liabilities; NET CURRENT ASSETS is the difference between the current assets and the current liabilities.

Liabilities are valued at the amounts expected to be paid at the expected maturity date. In some cases, amounts that are not quite certain will be included as liabilities; they will be valued at the best estimate available. The convention of CONSERVATISM suggests that amounts that are reasonably likely to be liabilities should be treated thus. Less likely amounts are called CONTINGENCIES.

LIFO (last in, first out). – one of the methods available for the calculation of the cost of INVENTORIES (stocks), in those frequent cases where it is difficult or impossible to determine exactly which items remain or have been used. When prices are rising, LIFO will lead to more up-to-date values for the use of inventory (COST OF SALES) and, thus, lower profits. Therefore, it is popular with many companies in the USA, where it is allowed for tax purposes (as long as it is also used in the income statement).

However, the inventory value shown in the BALANCE SHEET may be seriously misleading as it will be based on very old prices. Thus, the method is discouraged by the appropriate ACCOUNTING STANDARD (SSAP 9) in the UK, and is rarely found. Nevertheless it is allowed by the Companies Acts; though it is not accepted for tax purposes.

For a simple numerical example, see FIFO.

Limited liability companies. – companies whose owners have limited liability for the debts of their businesses. The owners of partnerships and sole trader businesses are fully liable in law for the debts of those businesses. Thus, the providers of ownership finance for such businesses tend to be few in number, and restricted to those who are able and willing to become managers of the business in order to protect their interests.

For really large businesses with thousands of owners another legal form is necessary, so that the owners (or shareholders) may have limited liability for the debts of their business, and therefore be prepared to delegate management to directors. In 1855 in the UK a Companies Act introduced the possibility of registration of companies in limited liability form.

The liability of shareholders is limited to their share capital. Of course, this may damage the interests of lenders. Thus, companies are forced to disclose annual audited information, are generally not allowed to pay back capital to shareholders, and have to notify lenders of their status by putting after their names some such warnings as Ltd, plc (UK) or Ltd, Inc (US). For equivalent names in some other countries, see COMPANIES.

Liquidity. – the short-run financial health of a business. Poor liquidity may lead to difficulties in paying debts as they fall due, and to inability to undertake profitable projects due to lack of funds. Of course, it may be possible to solve this in the long run by being profitable; or in the short run by selling assets or by issuing more shares or long-term loan stock.

One measure of liquidity is the NET CURRENT ASSETS or working capital of a business, which is the current assets less the current liabilities. Other measures include the liquidity ratios: the CURRENT RATIO and the QUICK RATIO (Acid Test). However, all these measures are most useful when seen in the context of similar companies and when one can look at a trend for a particular company.

Listed companies. – companies listed or quoted on a STOCK EXCHANGE. This means that there is an organized and substantial market in their shares, such that one can always buy or sell them. Stock Exchanges have 'listing requirements' concerning behaviour and the financial disclosures that companies must make.

In order to be listed, a company must be a public limited company (plc) in the UK, or registered with the SEC in the USA. In both countries, there are many public or registered companies that are not listed. Such unlisted companies may have decided to be public so that their shares may be bought and sold in less major markets than Stock Exchanges.

The entry for STOCK EXCHANGES has some details of the numbers of listed companies in different countries.

Loan capital. There are many expressions used in the UK and the USA for long-term loans: debt capital, loan stock, DEBENTURES, fixed interest capital. Loans may be made by private persons, other businesses or banks. In many cases, there is a market in loan securities, so that they can be sold to other investors by the original lender. The loans will usually have a fixed repayment, redemption or maturity date, and a fixed interest entitlement until that date.

Loans will normally be recorded in the borrowing company's BALANCE SHEET at the repayment amount, as long-term liabilities. However, their value in the securities market at any moment will depend upon their interest rate and maturity date, and upon the market rate of interest at that moment.

Lower of cost and market. – a well-established rule for the valuation of CURRENT ASSETS, particularly INVENTORIES (US)/stocks (UK). In conventional accounting, 'cost' means the historical purchase price of the inventory, plus the costs of work done on it. In the UK, 'market value' means NET REALIZABLE VALUE (NRV), which is what the stock could be sold for in the normal course of business when ready for sale (less any expected costs involved in finishing and selling it). In the USA, 'market value' can also mean the replacement cost of the inventory, where this is lower than the NRV.

The reason for this rule is CONSERVATISM. This suggests that, since the business intends to sell the inventory fairly soon, its value should not be held above its expected selling price. On the other hand, it should also not be held above its cost, as with other assets under the historical cost convention. Normally, particularly if prices are rising, cost will be used, because it will be below NRV.

For fixed assets, which the business does not intend to sell, the NRV is normally ignored in favour of the historical cost.

M

Mainstream corporation tax. – an element of the UK tax system since 1973; MCT is the amount of the corporation tax liability (CTL) for a year that has not already been paid as the ADVANCE CORPORATION TAX (ACT) connected to a divided payment. Thus, MCT = CTL – ACT. The MCT is paid between 9 and 21 months after a company's year end; the timing depends on the date of formation and the accounting year end of a company. MCT is not allowed to fall below zero.

Management accounting. – may be distinguished from other work done by accountants, like auditing or financial accounting, in that it is designed specifically to serve the needs of the managers of a business. Financial accounting and reporting is required by law or government bodies and is intended for shareholders and creditors. Thus, it has to obey many rules and has to strive for objectivity. Management accounting can be tailor-made for a particular company and will involve many estimates and forecasts.

Management accounting information will be designed to aid decision-making and planning. The information will be intended to be more detailed, frequent, prompt and future-oriented than financial accounting. Management accounting may include COST ACCOUNTING, BUDGETS, investment appraisal and long-range planning.

Management buy-out. – the purchase of a company, as a going concern, by members of its management. This became a popular activity in the UK in the early 1980s. A company might decide that it (or one of its subsidiaries) was not sufficiently profitable or that there were insufficient resources to continue in business. In some such cases, few potential buyers could be found; and closing down could be very expensive in terms of redundancy payments and loss of value of assets (due to low break-up values compared to values-in-use). Often, the most logical purchasers are a consortium of managers: they know the business, they can reduce the redundancy costs and they want to stay in work in the same location. There are many examples of success of this arrangement, partly due to the added drive and enthusiasm of a workforce that owns its own business.

Management letter. – a letter from the auditors of a company to its managers concerning the adequacy of control systems, the efficiency of management, etc. In the UK and the USA, the report of the auditors on the annual financial statements is normally very brief and standardized. It is not a report on the above matters but on the fairness of the financial statements. However, the auditors will have investigated control systems and efficiency to some extent, and may have noticed problems during their work. As part of the normal audit procedure, they will send the private 'management letter' to the board of directors of the audited company, detailing any problems foreseen or areas of weakness of control.

Marginal cost. – the extra cost that would result from producing one extra unit of a product (strictly, an infinitesimally small amount extra). The marginal cost must be set in the context of an existing level of production. It might well cost more to move from a steady production of 1000 per week to 1001 per week, than to move from one million per week to one million and one.

For the purpose of calculating marginal cost, all the fixed costs should be ignored; only those extra costs that are strictly related to the small production increase should be measured. For decision-making purposes, it is often useful to compare the marginal cost of extra production with the marginal revenue that would result.

Market capitalization. – the total value of the shares of a company at a particular moment, as found by multiplying the number of its shares by the market price. In some newspapers, market capitalization is published, next to share prices.

Of course, if one owned all the shares, one could probably not sell them all for the capitalization thus suggested. As soon as one began to sell large numbers, the price might fall.

Matching. – a convention that the expenses and revenues measured in order to calculate the profit for a period should be those that relate to the period, rather than those where cash has been paid or received. This is sometimes called the accruals convention.

For example, accountants record a sale on credit when it would be legally enforceable or on delivery of goods, not at the later date when cash is received. Similarly, the electricity expense of a business will be the amount that *relates* to the period, not what happened to be paid in the period. DEPRECIATION is a good example of the matching concept in action. When a fixed asset is bought, it will normally be used for several years. Thus, accountants do not charge an expense equal to the cost of the asset in the year of purchase. Instead, the asset is 'capitalized' and recorded in the BALANCE SHEET; and it is gradually charged as an expense, called depreciation, over the years of its use.

The main problem with the widespread use of this concept is the number of estimations involved. This adds subjectivity to accounting, even to an otherwise fairly objective system like HISTORICAL COST ACCOUNTING.

Materiality. – a very strong concept in ANGLO-SAXON ACCOUNTING, that rules should not be strictly applied to unimportant amounts. For example, some companies may have very small amounts of a particular revenue, expense, asset or liability; if such an account would normally be shown in the financial statements, it need not be shown if it is immaterial in size. This will help to make the statements clearer, by omission of trivial amounts. Materiality is also to be seen at work in the extensive rounding of numbers in financial statements.

Similarly, a strictly correct measurement or valuation method may be ignored for immaterial items. For example, the fitting of new and improved door locks on an office building is strictly an enhancement of the building and should lead to that asset being shown at a higher cost in the balance sheet. However, the cost will be immaterial in the context of the building, and capitalization would complicate future depreciation charges. Thus, it would be normal to treat the new locks as an expense.

There is no precise definition of what is material, just as there is no definition of how to achieve FAIR PRESENTATION. However, an item is immaterial if omission or mistreatment of it would not alter a reader's assessment of the financial statements. As a rule of thumb, this might be expressed as a few per cent of turnover or profit.

Materiality overrides other accounting rules most of the time. However, it is not so well developed in continental European countries.

Memorandum of association. – a legal document drawn up as part of the registration of a company in the UK. The US equivalent is the CERTIFICATE OF INCORPORATION. The memorandum includes a record of the company's name, its registered office, its purposes and its AUTHORIZED SHARE CAPITAL.

The other document drawn up at the birth of a UK company is the ARTICLES OF ASSOCIATION. These are rules concerning the relationships of the company to the shareholders, the shareholders to each other, and so on.

Merger accounting. – a method of accounting for a business combination. In the USA it is in frequent use, under the name of POOLING OF INTERESTS, under which heading more details may be found.

In the UK, it has been normal to use the acquisition method for business combinations and the subsequent preparation of CONSOLIDATED FINANCIAL STATEMENTS. That method involves the bringing in of the taken-over assets at fair values at the date of acquisition, and the valuation at market prices of any shares exchanged as part of the purchase price.

However, the merger method brings in the assets at original historical cost; and the shares are valued at PAR VALUE. Merger accounting was thought to be illegal under the 1948 Companies Act; and this was confirmed in a legal case, Shearer v Bercain, of 1980. However, the 1981 Companies Act legalized the method, and SSAP 23 outlines the details.

We can expect to see more of the merger method in the UK for those mergers where 90 per cent or more of the consideration passes in the form of shares rather than cash.

Minority interests. – the capital provided by, and earned for, group shareholders who are not parent company shareholders. Many subsidiary companies are not fully owned by the parent company. This means that they are partly owned by 'minority' shareholders outside the group. In the preparation of CONSOLIDATED FINANCIAL STATEMENTS, accountants bring in 100 per cent of all assets, liabilities, expenses and revenues of subsidiaries. This is because the group fully *controls* the subsidiary, even if it does not fully own it. In such financial statements, the subsidiary is submerged into the rest of the group, and the capital provided by the minority shareholders is separately recognized as part of the capital of the group called 'minority interests'. This amount grows each time the relevant subsidiary makes a profit that is not distributed.

In the consolidated profit and loss account, the share of the group profit owned by minorities is also shown, as 'profit attributable to minorities'.

Monetary assets. – those assets that are denominated in money terms or have a 'face value'. Cash or DEBTORS (UK)/ACCOUNTS RECEIVABLE (US) are examples of monetary assets. Non-monetary assets include land, buildings and equipment. The distinction between monetary and non-monetary assets is important for some systems of FOREIGN CURRENCY TRANSLATION and of INFLATION ACCOUNTING.

Monetary working capital adjustment (MWCA). – one of the adjustments made to HISTORICAL COST ACCOUNTING profit in certain systems of CURRENT COST ACCOUNTING (CCA) in order to take account of changing prices. It is designed to adjust for the extra money tied up in trade DEBTORS (net of trade CREDITORS) as a result of the rise in price of stocks (inventories). If prices are rising, the MWCA would be a DEBIT, an extra charge against profit. However, it would work equally well in reverse, if prices fell.

The CCA system of 1980 to 1985 in the UK, as required for large and listed companies by ACCOUNTING STANDARD SSAP 16, contained an MWCA. The successor system is also designed to contain one.

Money measurement convention. Traditionally, accountants only include items in accounts and financial statements that can be measured in money terms with reasonable objectivity. Thus, the value of a skilled management team or loyal staff or the goodwill of customers is not normally shown in financial statements. This is because it is difficult to measure its worth in money terms.

This convention is linked to the use of HISTORICAL COST ACCOUNTING, where assets are measured at their purchase price or production cost.

Mutual funds. – US name for financial institutions that use money provided by investors to own and manage a portfolio of investment in other stocks and shares. The UK equivalents are UNIT TRUSTS.

N

Netherlands. Financial reporting in the Netherlands is quite unlike that in the neighbouring continental countries, where there is a tradition based on conservatism, detailed rules and the dominance of taxation. Dutch accounting is more like that in the Anglo-Saxon world, where a strong body of professional accountants makes the detailed rules, and strives to give a fair presentation in financial statements.

This similarity to UK accounting may be due to the mercantile and laissez-faire past of the Netherlands. However, in the twentieth century, a clearer influence has been the teachings of Professor Limperg of Amsterdam. From him comes a strong tradition of fair presentation based on REPLACEMENT COST information. Some companies have published replacement cost financial statements for many years; for example, Philips since 1951. Nevertheless, full use of replacement cost is certainly a minority practice.

The important influences in Dutch accounting are the Guidelines set by a body that includes the Netherlands Institute of Registered Accountants; the Enterprise Chamber of the High Court, which hears cases against companies; and the Companies Acts, including that of 1983 which implemented the EEC's FOURTH DIRECTIVE.

Net assets. – the worth of a business in accounting terms, as measured from its BALANCE SHEET. That is, it is the total of all the assets, less the liabilities that are owed to outsiders. Naturally, this total equals the SHAREHOLDERS' EQUITY.

However, in reality, a business is nearly always worth more that its net assets, because accountants will have been using HISTORICAL COST ACCOUNTING as a measurement basis, and because important assets like the goodwill of customers will have been excluded due to the CONSERVATISM and MONEY MEASUREMENT conventions. Thus, the MARKET CAPITALIZATION of a company will nearly always be greater than its accounting 'net assets'.

Net book value (NBV). – the amount at which an asset is held in the accounts of a business. This will depend upon the system of accounting being used, and is unlikely to be directly related to what the asset could be sold for. Conventional accounting measures assets at their net historical cost of purchase or production. The reason for the word 'net' is that most fixed assets are gradually written off over their useful lives by amounts of DEPRECIATION. Thus, the NBV is usually the historical cost less accumulated charges of depreciation. It is the NBV that is recorded on a BALANCE SHEET.

In the UK, it is fairly common for companies to revalue land and buildings from time to time. This will affect the NBV.

Net current assets. The net current assets or working capital of a business is the excess of the CURRENT ASSETS (like cash, INVENTORIES and DEBTORS/ACCOUNTS RECEIVABLE) over the CURRENT LIABILITIES (like trade creditors and overdrafts).

This is a measure of the extent to which the business is safe from liquidity problems. However, the movement of the total from year to year, or the CURRENT RATIO (of current assets to current liabilities) might be more useful information.

Net income. – normal US expression for NET PROFIT in UK terminology.

Net present value (NPV). – normally used in the context of the NPV method of investment appraisal, which compares projects (or judges the likely success of one project) by estimating all the future net cash flows that would result from them, including the initial investment as an outflow and any investment incentives as inflows. These flows are 'discounted' to take account of the fact that money *now* is worth more than money *later*. Thus, the method involves estimation of a discount rate and of many years' worth of future cash inflows and outflows.

The NPV method is regarded as theoretically superior to others, such as the simple PAY-BACK METHOD that ignores the time value of money and the cash flows after the pay-back period. However, the latter is much more popular, perhaps because it is easier to use and to explain to non-financial managers. It is sometimes said that the pay-back method is preferable when uncertainty is great, but the NPV can take account of this by using a higher discount rate.

Net profit. – the excess of all the REVENUES over all the EXPENSES of a business for a period. The PROFIT AND LOSS ACCOUNT of a business will show the net profit before tax and the net profit after tax. The profit is then available for distribution as dividends (assuming there is sufficient cash) or for transfer to various RESERVES. After any dividends on PREFERENCE SHARES have been deducted but before any EXTRAORDINARY ITEMS have been included, the figure may be called EARNINGS.

One measure of the success of a business is its PROFITABILITY, which may be calculated as a ratio of net profit before interest and tax to NET ASSETS, or as a ratio of net profit after interest and tax to SHAREHOLDERS' EQUITY.

Net realizable value (NRV). – the amount that could be raised by selling an asset, less the costs of the sale. Normally, NRV implies a sale in the normal course of trade; thus, there would also be a deduction for any costs to bring the asset into a saleable state.

The normal rule for the valuation of CURRENT ASSETS, like INVENTORIES, is to use the 'lower of cost and market', where the latter means the NRV (except that, in the USA, it can mean the replacement cost, where lower).

The use of NRV has also been proposed for some systems of INFLATION ACCOUNTING, either as the main valuation basis or as a basis for those assets that are about to be sold.

Net worth. – a term equivalent to NET ASSETS. It means the total of the assets less the liabilities due to outsiders. It is thus equal to SHAREHOLDERS' EQUITY. See NET ASSETS for further description.

New Zealand. Accounting and financial reporting in New Zealand is very similar to that in the UK. There is a fairly strong profession, whose members belong mainly to the New Zealand Society of Accountants; there are ACCOUNTING STANDARDS that are very similar to those of the UK; and there are Companies Acts like those of 1948 and 1967 in the UK, but not the standardized formats and accounting principles introduced by the UK's 1981 Companies Act.

Nominal ledger. – an expression that tends to be used now to mean the main BOOKS of account in which are stored the DOUBLE ENTRY records of the business. Originally, the only records kept would have related to amounts owed to or by persons. These would have been recorded on pieces of paper in a 'personal ledger'. Later, there would have been records of land and property in the 'real ledger'; and of things that were 'accounts' in name only, like interest or electricity expenses, in the nominal ledger. However, the term 'nominal ledger' has now supplanted the others in the UK; and it remains in use even where all the information is actually on a computer tape not in a big black book.

Nominal value. All shares in the UK and most of those in the USA have a nominal or par value. This is little more than a label to distinguish a share from any of a different type issued by the same company. Normally, the shares will be currently exchanged at above the nominal value, and the company will consequently issue any new shares at approximately the market price.

Dividends are expressed as a percentage of nominal value; and share capital is recorded at nominal value, any excess being recorded as SHARE PREMIUM (UK)/PAID-IN SURPLUS (US).

Non-business organizations. – US expression for what are called NOT-FOR-PROFIT organizations in the UK.

Notes to the financial statements. The main financial statements in a company's ANNUAL REPORT now contain a large number of figures, possibly too many for easy interpretation. However, there would be many times more information on the face of the financial statements had it not become standard practice to present details in the 'notes'. For example, the balance sheet will normally show only a few sub-totals for the various types of FIXED ASSETS (property, plant and equipment). In the notes will be found more detail of depreciation, disposals, additions, leased assets, and so on.

As far as law, ACCOUNTING STANDARDS or AUDIT are concerned, the notes form part of the financial statements. Many items are shown in the notes by some companies, but on the face of the financial statements by others.

Most of the details found in the notes are required to be disclosed by law, accounting standards or Stock Exchange requirements.

Not-for-profit. – an organization whose main aims are not commercial; for example, a university or a charity. Depending on the legal structure of such bodies, they may not be subject to normal accounting rules, though they may well be subject to other special rules. The US term is normally 'non-business organization'.

Such an organization will usually prepare a BALANCE SHEET, but will not prepare a PROFIT AND LOSS ACCOUNT (UK). It may instead prepare an INCOME AND EXPENDITURE ACCOUNT which still uses the MATCHING convention and other normal accounting rules, but arrives at a surplus or deficit rather than a profit or loss. Alternatively, it may abandon the matching convention in favour of cash accounting, when it will prepare a RECEIPTS AND PAYMENTS ACCOUNT.

O

Objectivity. An accounting measurement is said to be 'objective' if it is reasonably independent of the judgement of accountants. There is much to be said for objectivity in accounting, because this reduces the time taken to arrive at figures, and the time taken to check them. It also means that the readers of financial statements can be more easily reassured that the figures contained are not arbitrary.

The most obvious result of this desire for a simple, checkable system is the conventional use of HISTORICAL COST ACCOUNTING. The original purchase price of an asset is much more objective than its current selling price, replacement cost or the value of future benefits expected to flow from it. However, such techniques as DEPRECIATION and PROVISIONS (allowances) for bad debts do add subjectivity, even to historical cost accounting.

The main problem with greater objectivity is the possible sacrifice of relevance. The price of a machine eight years ago is objective, but irrelevant for a knowledge about how much the machine is worth or a decision about what to do with it.

A well-known saying in accounting is that it may be better to be approximately right than precisely wrong. Nevertheless, at present, most of the world settles for a system that might be said to be not even precisely wrong.

Off-balance-sheet finance. The main example of off-balance-sheet finance is the existence of finance LEASES that are not treated as assets and liabilities (capitalized). Suppose that a business has decided to lease most of its plant and equipment rather than buying it. Suppose, too, that it does not capitalize its leases, because it or its leases fall outside the rules or because it is in a country where capitalization is not required. Now, let us compare this company with a similar one that has borrowed money and bought all its assets. The lessee has few assets and few loans, whereas the buying company has many assets and many loans. Thus the lessee will appear to have a much better GEARING/leverage position and a better return on capital. This is despite the fact that it is using the same amount of assets, and has contracted to make lease payments for many future years.

In the USA and the UK, it is now necessary for 'capital' or 'finance' leases to be capitalized as though owned, and for an equal liability to be created. This adjusts for the otherwise misleading off-balance-sheet finance. It expresses SUBSTANCE OVER FORM and is an attempt to achieve FAIR PRESENTATION.

Oil and gas accounting. There has been much controversy in the USA about how to account for oil and gas exploration and discoveries. In the

UK, surprisingly little official attention has been given to the subject, considering its importance to the economy.

In the USA, an ACCOUNTING STANDARD of 1977 (SFAS 19, withdrawn in 1979) required the use of the 'successful efforts' method; a conservative method in which only the costs of drilling worthwhile holes are treated as assets (capitalized). However, after complaints from oil companies, the SECURITIES AND EXCHANGE COMMISSION (SEC) intervened in 1978 in order to allow the 'full cost' method, in which the costs of related, but unsuccessful, explorations are also capitalized. The SEC also called for the development of an accounting method that would give a better reflection of the value of the discovered resources: 'reserve recognition accounting' (RRA). The search for an acceptable method of RRA appears to have been abandoned now. Meanwhile, the FASB has issued standards calling for disclosures of current cost and reserve information.

In the UK, there are no standards or laws on the appropriate method. Companies choose what they consider to be the most appropriate: mostly the full cost or successful efforts methods.

Operating income/profit. 'Operating income' means different things in different contexts. In conventional, HISTORICAL COST ACCOUNTING, it usually means the profit before the deduction of interest and tax, and possibly excluding gains from the letting of property or the sale of used machines. However, in the context of INFLATION ACCOUNTING, 'operating profit' may mean something more complicated; that is, the historical cost profit, before interest and tax, adjusted for the effects of price changes on depreciation, cost of sales and, possibly, monetary working capital.

Opportunity cost. – a concept beloved of most economists and many accountants. The opportunity cost of doing something is the best alternative thereby forgone. For example, if a business has spare cash, it might appear to be costless to use it for a new project. However, when evaluating the viability of the project, managers should put in a charge for the forgone interest or returns from alternative projects.

On the other hand, consider factories or staff that are standing idle and yet, for various reasons, are not to be dispensed with by the business. Suppose that no use for them has been available, until a new project is dreamt up. It would not be sensible to consider the depreciation or rates of the factory when deciding whether to carry out the project; those costs would be incurred anyway. Thus, it may be that the opportunity cost of the assets is zero, and that this is the more sensible figure for decision-making.

Ordinary shares. – UK expression for the main type of ownership capital of companies. The US equivalent is 'common stock'.

In the UK, shares are issued with a nominal or PAR VALUE, which is little more than a label to distinguish one sort of share from another. The very first issue of shares may be made at the nominal value, but later new issues will be made at the highest price expected to be acceptable in the market. In a BALANCE SHEET, the amount of money contributed by shareholders is split into issued share capital (at nominal values) and SHARE PREMIUM (for the excess amounts).

A company will also have an AUTHORIZED SHARE CAPITAL, as specified in its MEMORANDUM of association. This is a maximum potential share capital, which is disclosed as a note to the balance sheet.

The main alternative type of share capital is PREFERENCE SHARES, but these have been unpopular since 1965 due to a change in the tax system.

Overheads. – expenses of a business that cannot readily be traced to units of production or processes that produce particular single products. The term INDIRECT COSTS has the same meaning. Obvious examples of overheads include the computer of the administration, the salaries of factory managers, and the property taxes on the company's buildings. There will be production overheads, administration overheads, distribution overheads, and possibly others.

When calculating the net profit of the whole business, these costs must obviously be included. However, for making decisions about which types of production to expand or contract, it is usually difficult to feel certain about any allocation of overheads to particular products. This leads some businesses to make some decisions on the basis of direct costs only; this may be called variable costing or marginal costing. The full allocation of overhead costs to products is called absorption costing.

Over-the-counter securities. – a method of allowing the exchange of securities for those companies that are not large enough for a full listing on a Stock Exchange, or for companies who would prefer not to obey the 'listing requirements' of an Exchange.

In the USA, not all OTC companies have to be registered with the SECURITIES AND EXCHANGE COMMISSION; only those with 500 or more shareholders and $1m or more assets.

Own shares. Until the 1981 Companies Act, it was not possible for a UK company to purchase back its own ordinary shares from its shareholders. That rule was designed to protect creditors. However, many countries did allow this; in the USA, own shares may be held by a company and are called TREASURY STOCK. The UK joined the others, partly in order to allow private companies to buy out 'troublesome minorities' of their shareholders who could not find buyers.

When own shares are bought back, a transfer of distributable profit must be made to an undistributable CAPITAL REDEMPTION RESERVE; this fulfils the function of protecting the creditors. The worst complications are perhaps those of taxation, which are dealt with in the 1982 Finance Act.

P

Pacioli, Luca. Fra Luca Pacioli is the most famous man in the history of accounting. He lived between about 1445 and about 1513. He was professor of mathematics at various Italian universities, and was a Franciscan friar (hence the 'Fra' for fratello, i.e. brother). He was a friend of popes, princes and artists, including Leonardo da Vinci who drew the famous 'proportions of man' as an illustration for one of Pacioli's books.

His is the earliest surviving major treatise on DOUBLE ENTRY. It may be found in a book published in Venice in 1494, *Summa de Arithmetica, Geometria, Proportioni et Proportionalità.* This work had immense influence on the spread of double entry, as it was gradually adapted into several languages. Pacioli was certainly not the inventor of double entry (by about 200 years) but his book did much to popularize it.

'. . . and the cell with a double entry is Pacioli's'

Paid-in surplus. – US expression for part of the amounts of money paid by investors when they purchased a company's shares. Most shares in the USA have a PAR VALUE, which is a sort of label. Usually, shares are issued at above par value, in which case the capital paid in is divided into share capital (at par) and paid-in surplus (the excess above par). For most purposes, paid-in surplus is treated exactly as if it were 'share capital'.

There are several alternative titles for these amounts, including 'paid-in capital'. In the UK, the equivalent term is SHARE PREMIUM.

Par value. – the normal US expression for the label attached to a share, that helps to distinguish it from other types of share of the same company. The term is also used in the UK, where 'nominal value' is an equivalent expression. Share capital is recorded 'at par', although the issue price, after the company is formed, is usually in excess of par, because the market price for existing shares will usually be higher. The excess amounts over par are called PAID-IN SURPLUS (US)/SHARE PREMIUM (UK).

Dividends may be expressed in terms of a percentage of par value. All UK shares, but not all US shares, have a par value.

Parent company. – generally, a company that owns more than 50 per cent of the shares of another company (its subsidiary). The normal financial reporting treatment is to prepare CONSOLIDATED FINANCIAL STATEMENTS for the group containing the parent and the subsidiaries. For this purpose, certain subsidiaries would be excluded: in the USA, financial institutions would be omitted from groups that were mainly operating in other fields; subsidiaries may also be excluded if control is restricted or temporary.

Partnership. – a business entity whereby several persons pool their capital and skills, and share the risks and profits. Normally, most or all of the partners are directly involved in the management of the business, unlike many companies where most shareholders are not part of management. In the UK and the USA, partners are fully liable (do not have LIMITED LIABILITY) for the debts of the business, which is partly why they all wish to be involved in the management. Also, in the USA and the UK except for Scotland, partnerships are not legal entities; one would have to take the partners not the partnership to court. In continental Europe, there are several different forms of partnership, and they do have legal personality.

In the UK, most partnerships are limited to 20 partners by law. Thus, larger businesses become companies, who may also find limited liability an essential feature for raising large amounts of capital. However, for certain professions, like accountancy and law, the limit on the number of partners is removed. This fits in with the prohibition by the professional bodies on the formation of professional companies, which is designed to ensure that professionals act responsibly, because of their unlimited liability.

Patent. – the exclusive right to use a product or process which, when successfully registered, may be an exceptionally valuable asset. However, its value is very hard to quantify because it rests upon future income streams. Thus, accountants, who like to preserve as much OBJECTIVITY as possible, normally value patents at their purchase price or production cost. The latter would include those costs attributable to the invention of the patented product or process. Patents are subject to DEPRECIATION (or amortization) over their useful lives. Patents are classified as INTANGIBLE ASSETS.

Pay-back method. – a popular technique for appraising the likely success of projects, or for choosing between projects. It involves the analysis of their expected future net cash inflows, followed by a calculation of how many years it will take for the original capital investment to be recovered. It seems to be popular because it is simple to use and, perhaps more importantly, simple to explain to non-financial managers.

It may give a reasonable answer when choosing between projects with similar expected patterns of cash flows and similar initial investments. However, several criticisms may be made about the more general use of it. First, the method ignores the net cash flows that arise after the pay-back period; the quicker pay-back project may actually be far less profitable in total. Second, the method ignores the time value of money; that is, it ignores the fact that money received in two years' time is less valuable than an equal amount received in one year's time.

More sophisticated methods of investment appraisal, like the NET PRESENT VALUE (NPV) method, adjust for both the above problems by discounting all the expected future income flows. However, these methods are not popular with businessmen, presumably because they are more difficult to understand, and involve many more judgements. The pay-back method is often used in conjunction with others.

Pension costs. Precisely how much a company should set aside for future pension payments to retired and present employees is a very complex matter. The calculations are performed by actuaries, who are often thought by accountants to be as clever and as expensive as computers but even more mystical.

Some pensions schemes work on a pay-as-you-go basis, whereby current payments by the company and employees into the pension funds are designed merely to pay current pensioners. However, CONSERVATISM and the MATCHING convention suggest that pension schemes should be 'fully funded', that is be capable of paying pension commitments that have so far built up for existing employees and pensioners.

In the mid-1980s, the bodies that set ACCOUNTING STANDARDS in the UK and the USA began to grapple seriously with the problem; exposure drafts and standards are being issued on disclosure and measurement problems. For some under-funded companies, massive payments into pension funds may become necessary.

Payments by companies and by employees into pension schemes are tax deductible.

Petroleum revenue tax (PRT). – a UK tax on oil companies. It is a well-known principle of fiscal authorities that anything profitable ought to be taxed. The development of North Sea oil production in the UK in the 1970s led to the introduction of PRT in 1975. This is a fairly complex tax, with several allowances for capital spending and small fields, and it has been changed several times since its introduction. PRT is an allowable expense against CORPORATION TAX, which is also paid by oil companies.

Plan comptable. An 'accounting plan' is the fundamental set of instructions for accounting practices in France, Belgium, Spain and some developing countries. In France the *plan comptable général* contains a standard decimalized CHART OF ACCOUNTS; the instructions relating to the presentation of uniform published financial statements; and standard definitions of items and their valuation methods. The chart of accounts is for internal use and for annual returns to the Ministry of Economics and Finance in Paris, where charts from all over France are collated in order to assist in centralized economic management.

The *plan comptable* was originally a German invention, introduced in France during the Second World War. However, it was seen as useful by the French, and has been used since, with revisions (1947, 1957, 1982). The 1982 revision came into operation for accounting years beginning on 1 January 1984; it contains the formats for published financial statements as required by the EEC's FOURTH DIRECTIVE.

The plan is controlled and revised by a government body, the *Conseil National de la Comptabilité*.

Pooling of interests. – a method of accounting for business combinations that is fairly common in the USA, and in occasional use in the UK, where it is known as MERGER ACCOUNTING. The method has several attractions to companies (explained below) and it is therefore necessary for there to be rules to control its use. In the USA, these rules are to be found in APB Opinion 16, and they include that the merger should be accomplished by the exchange of shares only, so that no cash leaves the group of companies.

Most business combinations do not fit within the rules, and so the normal 'acquisition' or 'purchase' method of preparing CONSOLIDATED FINANCIAL STATEMENTS is used. This method involves the bringing in of the assets of the subsidiaries at fair values at the date of acquisition of the subsidiaries, and the valuation of any shares exchanged in the purchase at market values. This will normally lead to the recognition of large amounts of GOODWILL on consolidation.

By contrast, the pooling-of-interests method values assets and shares at their existing book values (usually historical cost for assets and PAR

VALUE for shares). There will be no goodwill, which will remove the need to depreciate it. The method also adds together the reserves of the merged companies, whereas purchase accounting includes only the post-acquisition reserves of subsidiaries as reserves of the group. In summary, the pooling of interests method treats the merged companies as if they had always been one company.

Post balance sheet events. A balance sheet is drawn up at a particular point in time, perhaps December 31 each year. Thus, the events that occur after that date might be thought to be irrelevant in the presentation of a balance sheet. However, events of material size may be included in one of two ways, assuming that they happen before the balance sheet is finalized by the company and its auditors.

First, something may happen that makes clear a situation that already existed at the balance sheet date. For example, a doubtful debt may prove good after all. In such a case, the unnecessary provision for doubtful debts can be written back to profit. Secondly, there may be an event that would affect the interpretation given to the financial statements. For example, several of the company's buildings may burn down after the balance sheet date. Such an event would not cause an adjustment to the financial statements, but would be recorded in the notes to them.

The UK rules for this can be found in SSAP 17.

Pre-acquisition profits. – undistributed profits of a subsidiary company that had been earned before the company was purchased by its present parent company. Thus, they are not seen as reserves of that group in CONSOLIDATED FINANCIAL STATEMENTS. Group reserves are calculated as the undistributed profits of the parent company, plus the group's share of undistributed post-acquisition profits of the consolidated companies.

In the case of companies dealt with by the minority practice of POOLING OF INTERESTS (US)/MERGER ACCOUNTING (UK), all reserves can be included in group reserves because the group companies are treated as if they had always been part of the group.

Preference shares/preferred stock. A minority of shares in some companies are issued as preference shares (UK) or preferred stock (US). These shares normally have preference over ordinary shares/common stock for dividend payments and for the return of capital if a company is wound up. That is, ordinary/common dividends cannot be paid in a particular year until the preference/preferred dividend, which is usually a fixed percentage, has been paid. Further, it is usual for preference/preferred shares to be 'cumulative', that is for any unpaid dividends to cumulate into future years and to remain preferential to any ordinary/common dividend.

The disadvantage to shareholders is that, if a company is successful, the ordinary/common dividend will be expected to rise over the years, whereas the preference/preferred dividend will not.

Tax changes in the UK in 1965 made preference shares much less attractive than fixed interest loans, because the interest on the latter is tax deductible for companies whereas dividends are not. Thus, preference share capital has become quite rare.

Preliminary expenses. The expenses relating to the setting up of a company, such as those relating to the issue of shares or the preparation of legal documents, are not allowed to be capitalized (shown as ASSETS) in either the UK or the USA. They must thus be treated as expenses immediately.

In some other countries, such as France, such expenses can be capitalized as assets and gradually depreciated.

Prepayments. – amounts recorded in a BALANCE SHEET which show that certain payments have been made in advance; perhaps for rents, property taxes or insurance premiums. Conventional accounting uses the accruals or MATCHING principle which is that only the expenses that *relate* to a period should be charged against profit for that period. Thus, prepayments will have been paid in the period leading up to the balance sheet, but will not be treated as expenses until a subsequent period. Technically, instead of the DEBIT being treated as an expense, it is treated as an asset.

The parallel treatment for expenses paid late gives rise to 'accrued expenses' on the balance sheet.

Present value. – the future net cash inflows expected from an asset or a proposed project, 'discounted' to reflect the fact that money is more valuable if received now rather than later. For the valuation of an asset, it might be more normal to refer to the method as the 'economic value'; this makes an appearance as a possible valuation under unusual circumstances under some systems of INFLATION ACCOUNTING. When choosing between investment projects, these concepts are normally considered under the heading of NET PRESENT VALUE (NPV).

Price/earnings ratio. The P/E ratio has become exceptionally important in the late 20th century as a rapid means of summing up the way in which investors view a particular company. The ratio at any moment compares the market price of an ordinary/common share in the company with the EARNINGS PER SHARE (EPS) of that company, based on the most recently available year's figure for the profit after interest, tax and preference/preferred dividend, but before EXTRAORDINARY ITEMS.

A high P/E means that a share is expected to perform well in the future. Investors must deem it to be worth paying a large multiple of the earnings for the share, because of their high expectations. However, this does not help one to decide which share to buy; it merely shows one which shares are well thought of: they are of course more expensive. For large Stock Exchanges, like those of London and New York, there is considerable evidence that available information is rapidly taken into account in share prices (this is called the efficient market hypothesis). Thus, there should be no share that is obvious 'good value': good shares will command good prices.

Prior-year adjustments. – may come about if a business discovers an error of material size in its financial statements of previous years, or if there is a change in accounting policies due to new laws, standards or circumstances. It is UK practice, under SSAP 6, to adjust the balance sheet of the previous year to take account of such events. This is because any changes that result are deemed not to be economic events of the current year, and thus not to be suitable items for a profit and loss account. In the USA, such items would be shown in the income statement of the year of their occurrence. In both countries, the notes to the financial statements would explain the accounting adjustments.

Private company. As registered under UK company law, a private company is one that is not allowed to sell its shares or loan stock on an open market. Such companies have 'limited' or an abbreviation as part of their names, as opposed to 'public limited company' for PUBLIC COMPANIES. The vast majority of UK companies are private companies; there are about 900,000 of them.

The company law relating to private companies is slightly less onerous than that for public companies. For example, private companies under certain size limits are exempted from some annual publication requirements; and private companies have a slightly less restrictive definition of distributable profit.

Profit. – in accounting terms, the excess of the REVENUES over the EXPENSES of the period. The revenues and expenses are those that *relate* to the period, rather than necessarily those that were received or paid in cash in the period. That is, the MATCHING convention is followed. The term 'net income' is now more usual in the USA.

A summary of the items involved in the calculation of profit is shown on a profit and loss account (UK)/income statement (US). At various stages of the calculation, figures of GROSS PROFIT, NET PROFIT before tax, net profit after tax, and EARNINGS may be shown. Also, infrequent amounts that are outside the normal course of the business are disclosed as EXTRAORDINARY ITEMS.

The measurement of profit is by no means an exact science. It involves several estimated amounts, including DEPRECIATION of assets and PROVISIONS for bad debts. Further, there is much argument about whether and how to adjust accounting figures for changes in prices. The conventional system, HISTORICAL COST ACCOUNTING, makes no direct adjustment for this. Thus, the expenses of the using up of inventories (stocks) and of depreciation are based on out-of-date prices (see INFLATION ACCOUNTING).

It might be fair to say that the average accounting practitioner has little time for philosophy about the meaning of the concept of profit; and the standard-setting bodies and academic accountants have been unsuccessful so far in finding an acceptable definition.

Profit and loss account. – the UK expression for the financial statement that summarizes the difference between the revenues and expenses of a period. Such statements may be drawn up frequently for the managers of a business, but a full audited statement is normally only published for each accounting year. The equivalent US expression is 'income statement'.

Publication of profit and loss accounts was first made compulsory for companies in the UK by the 1929 Companies Act. There is now a choice of formats among the four set out in the 1985 Companies Act. It is normal for UK companies to choose a 'vertical' or 'statement' format, rather than a two-sided or 'account' format. For private companies below a certain size there are some exemptions from publication requirements, though not from audit or disclosure to shareholders. One of the basic UK formats is shown below.

D & D Pirana plc
Profit and Loss Account for Year Ending 198X (£000s)

Turnover		9000
Cost of sales		5800
Gross profit		3200
Distribution costs	400	
Administrative expenses	800	
Interest payable	500	1700
Net profit before tax		1500
Tax on profit on ordinary activities		700
Profit on ordinary activities after tax		800
Extraordinary loss after tax		50
Profit for the year		750
Dividends paid and proposed		200
Retained profit		550

Profitability. – not the same as the PROFIT of a business. A profit of a particular size may be impressive for a corner grocery shop, but unimpressive for a large multinational company. Measures of profitability try to put the profit into the context of the size of the business. Thus, profitability is normally a measure of the return on capital invested in the business. One possible ratio of profitability is of net profit before interest and tax *to* the total long-term finance of the business. Another ratio is the net profit after interest and tax *to* the shareholders' equity.

Such ratios become useful when one company can be compared to another or to the average for its industry; or when one company's ratio can be seen in the context of the ratios for previous years. In all cases, it is important to try to compare ratios that have been defined consistently.

Proportional consolidation. – a technique used in some countries as part of the preparation of CONSOLIDATED FINANCIAL STATEMENTS for a group of companies. It brings into the consolidated financial statements the group's share of all the assets, liabilities, revenues and expenses of the partly owned company. The method is virtually unknown in the UK and USA, but is used by companies in France for dealing with investments in companies that are held on a joint venture basis with one or more other investing companies.

Proprietary view. – a way of looking at companies that takes the point of view of the shareholders. The alternative point of view is to look at the company as an economic entity that has many providers of finance. This is called the entity view.

The view taken becomes important when choosing the exact method to use for the preparation of CONSOLIDATED FINANCIAL STATEMENTS. There seem to be elements of both stances in UK and US practice. Also, the choice of stance will affect preferences of capital maintenance concept for the choice between systems of INFLATION ACCOUNTING.

Prospectus. – a document, used by potential investors, that precedes the issue of shares to the public. It outlines the financial position and prospects of the company, and gives details of the senior executives. Assistance with the preparation of the document will usually have been sought from merchant bankers/investment bankers, and independent accountants will report on its reasonableness. A summary of previous years' financial results will also be included.

The Stock Exchanges and company law (UK)/Securities and Exchange Commission (US) lay down some rules for the content of prospectuses.

Provisions and reserves. Unfortunately, there is some vagueness about the use of these two words, despite definitions in UK company law. However, a provision in the UK usually means an amount charged against profit to reduce the recorded value of an asset or to cover an expected liability, even if the exact amount or timing of the liability is uncertain. A reserve, on the other hand, is an amount voluntarily or compulsorily set aside out of profit (after the latter has been calculated), often in order to demonstrate that the amount is not to be distributed as dividends (see RESERVES).

A company may have provisions for depreciation or for bad debts or for taxation or for law suits that are expected to go against the company. All these provisions, when they were set up or added to, would lead to a reduction in the reported profit figure. When the law suit is lost or the doubtful debt goes bad, the provision will be reduced, and no further charge against profit will be needed. Thus, CONSERVATISM will have ensured that losses are recognized as soon as they are anticipated rather than waiting until they occur.

Some potential losses are not at all likely, and it would be regarded as unduly conservative to make provisions for them. Instead they are recorded in the notes to the balance sheet as CONTINGENT LIABILITIES.

However, as mentioned above, usage of the words is loose. For example, it is not unknown for accountants and others to talk about a 'bad debt reserve'; and in some continental European countries there may be very large 'provisions for contingencies' that Anglo-Saxon practice would treat as reserves. In US terminology, 'allowance' is often used instead of 'provision', and an amount set aside to cover an expected liability would usually be called a reserve.

Prudence. – a concept that is very strong in the accounting practices of nearly all countries. As the term suggests, it implies being cautious in the valuation of assets or the measurement of profit. It means always taking the lowest reasonable estimate of the value of assets; always anticipating losses but never anticipating profits.

In the ACCOUNTING STANDARDS (SSAP 2) and company law of the UK, 'prudence' may be found as a compulsory, fundamental principle. However, the word CONSERVATISM is also in use, sometimes meaning a slightly stricter version of prudence.

In the USA, 'conservatism' is the word generally used for this concept. A lengthier discussion of its meaning can be found under that entry.

Public company. – a company whose securities (shares and loan stock) may be publicly traded. In the UK, the legal form of such a company is set out in the Companies Acts. The company must have 'public limited company' (or plc) as part of its name. There are equivalents to this form in other European countries (see COMPANIES); but in the USA the nearest equivalent is a corporation that is registered with the Securities and Exchange Commission.

In the UK, there are about 5,000 companies in the plc form, less than half of which are listed on the London Stock Exchange. Public companies have to obey slightly stricter rules than private companies. For example, there are no exemptions from the publication requirements of the Companies Acts, as apply to smaller private companies. Also, there is a slightly more restrictive definition of distributable profit.

Q

Qualified audit report. This does not refer to the qualifications of the auditors; although the UK Companies Acts and the SEC in the USA do indeed require companies to be audited by independent qualified accountants (see ACCOUNTANCY PROFESSION and AUDIT). A 'qualified' audit report is one which states that the financial statements give a true and fair view *except that* or *subject to* certain qualifying remarks.

The qualifications may concern the infringement of company law or ACCOUNTING STANDARDS. If there are sufficiently serious problems, the auditors may withhold their opinion (perhaps due to major uncertainties) or may give an adverse opinion.

Naturally, companies would much prefer to avoid any of the adverse publicity that might surround the absence of a 'clean' audit opinion. This may be a significant sanction that the auditors can use to bring about conformity with accounting standards. Some observers hold that the sanction of the company threatening to give the audit to another firm of auditors is more than countervailing!

Qualifying degrees. – those academic degrees that allow entry to training programmes or exemption from some examinations of professional accountancy bodies.

See RELEVANT DEGREES.

Quarterly reporting. Companies registered with the Securities and Exchange Commission in the USA (the approximate equivalent of public companies in the UK) are required to do more than present lavish disclosures in their annual reports. They also have to make quarterly reports on turnover and gross and net profit.

The closest UK parallel is the Stock Exchange requirement for unaudited interim (half-yearly) reports.

Quick ratio. A company's quick ratio (or 'acid test') is a measure of its liquidity. The ratio is normally measured by comparing the cash plus debtors (UK)/accounts receivable (US) of a company to its current liabilities. The latest available figures are used, normally those on the most recent balance sheet. In the case of the illustration in Figure 2 under the entry for BALANCE SHEET (where debtors are 1850, cash 300 and current liabilities 3500), the quick ratio would be $(300 + 1850) \div 3500 = 0.61$.

The cash and debtors/accounts receivable are said to be 'quick assets' because they are cash or near cash, unlike some inventories (stocks). Following this reasoning, an analyst may wish to omit bank overdrafts from the current liabilities, on the grounds that the former are not usually expected to be repaid very rapidly.

An alternative measure (of all current assets to all current liabilities) is called the CURRENT RATIO.

It is not useful to talk in terms of 'correct' levels for the current ratio or quick ratio. Any analysis of one company should involve comparison with similar companies or the whole industry to which the company belongs. Also, it may be useful to see a company's ratios in the context of a trend of a number of years.

Ratios can be too high as well as too low. A high ratio suggests cash standing idle or unnecessary amounts of other unproductive current assets. Of course, a low ratio suggests potential disaster in the shape of difficulties in paying one's bills/accounts as they fall due.

Quoted companies. – an alternative expression for listed companies, that is companies whose names appear on the list of a Stock Exchange. Such companies must be public limited companies in the UK, or registered with the Securities and Exchange Commission in the USA. For more details, see LISTED COMPANIES.

R

Random walk. What have the following in common: molecules in a cup of tea, tomorrow's weather, foreign currency exchange rates and share prices on a Stock Exchange? The answer appears to be that the short-term future movements of all these are not predictable; they move with a 'random walk', such that the best estimate of tomorrow's weather or of the price of BP shares is 'the same as today's'.

If it were possible to predict tomorrow's share prices accurately, then we would see predictors consistently making virtually unlimited amounts of money. Of course, once a significant number of predictors get in on the act, they will all be trying to buy the same shares; thus the price will rise *today* before consistent profits can be made, and this will re-establish tomorrow's price as unpredictable.

This idea is connected with the EFFICIENT MARKET HYPOTHESIS which regards share prices as rapidly taking into account any publicly available information; suggesting that one cannot consistently out-guess the market price, unless one is engaged upon illegal INSIDER DEALING.

Rate of return. – a measure of the profitability of a business; it normally compares the annual profit of the business with the amount of capital invested in it. The rate of return may be measured before tax or after tax; it is important to be clear on which one is concerned with. Such a measure will normally be used to compare one company with another. Thus, it is also important to define the profit figure and the capital or asset base carefully.

The *expected* rate of return may also be used as a yardstick to assess investment projects. For projects with similar expected lives and patterns of cash flow, this may be a useful method. Annual average rates of return may be the best figures to compare. However, the NET PRESENT VALUE (NPV) method is more sophisticated; and the PAY-BACK METHOD is easier to understand.

Ratios. Ratio analysis is a popular sport of investment analysts, financial journalists, text-book writers and examination setters. It involves the comparison of a company with its past or with other companies, by setting one piece of financial data in the context of another. Comparisons would be obviously meaningless if one looked at the absolute levels of profit for two companies of different sizes. However, they may be valuable when the profits of the two companies can be set in the context of their total assets or capital figures. This would lead to a comparison of profitability ratios.

Similarly, there are GEARING ratios that measure the proportion of debt finance; and liquidity ratios that measure the size of current assets in the context of the debts of a company. There is also the frequently used PRICE/EARNINGS RATIO, which sets the market price of an ordinary/common share in the context of its part of the annual earnings of the company.

Like most useful simplifications, ratio analysis contains great dangers. First, it is important to ensure that there is consistency of definition from year to year and from company to company. When international comparisons are being made, ratio analysis is especially dangerous, because there are major differences in the methods used for valuing assets and measuring profits.

Another danger is that 'ideal' ratios may be thought to exist. Let us take the liquidity ratio as an example. One can find textbooks that suggest that a CURRENT RATIO (i.e. current assets : current liabilities) should be above 2 : 1. However, it is nonsense to regard this as a general rule. For some companies in some industries (possibly heavy engineering), this level might be dangerously low; for other companies (supermarket chains) it would suggest exceptional inefficiency in the use of resources.

Real gains. Normally, the word 'real' in the context of accounting or economics implies an amount that has been corrected for inflation. Thus a 'real gain' is one that has been reduced to the extent that it is due merely to the change in value of money. See INFLATION ACCOUNTING.

Realizable profit. A profit is realizable, but unrealized, if productive activity or price rises mean that assets could be sold for more than they were previously recorded at in a company's accounts. Conventional HISTORICAL COST ACCOUNTING ignores realizable profits until they become objective and easily measurable by being realized, basically by sale. This is partly due to traditional CONSERVATISM, and partly to the much greater simplicity and auditability of objective, realized amounts.

However, the problem that results from this 'realization convention' is that the profits recorded for any year are a very incomplete indication of what happened in that year. To take a simple example, suppose that an asset is bought as an investment, and that it is sold after ten years. In the first nine years no gains will be recorded, but in the tenth year the full gain will be treated as profit even if the asset had actually lost value during the tenth year.

Systems of INFLATION ACCOUNTING try to correct for this problem in various ways.

Realization convention. – a well-established principle of conventional accounting, that gains or profits should only be recognized when they have been objectively realized by a sale being agreed. This is consistent with the all-pervasive concept of CONSERVATISM, which anticipates losses but never profits.

For example, suppose that the following facts relate to one job of a manufacturing company:

19 January	Buy raw materials, store them.
19 February	Begin work on processing the materials.
3 April	Finished goods produced and stored.
10 May	Customer orders goods and is invoiced.
17 May	Goods delivered.
5 June	Customer pays for the goods.

At what point is the revenue to be recognized? This question is especially important when the above cycle straddles an accounting end-of-period, as is frequently the case. By 3 April most of the work is done, but accountants would recognize no profit. They would wait until 10 May (or perhaps, in practice, 17 May) when a sale has been agreed. It would, of course, have been possible to invent an even more conservative system and to wait until the cash arrived on 5 June. Accountants cover the possibility that the debt will not be paid by making PROVISIONS for doubtful debts.

Certain proposed systems of INFLATION ACCOUNTING, notably continuously contemporary accounting (CoCoA), abandon the realization convention. However, in practice, the convention appears unassailable.

Realized profits. – profits that have been objectively verified by the evidence of a sale (see REALIZATION CONVENTION). Conventional accounting rests heavily upon the CONSERVATISM and objectivity that this enables. Company law in the UK requires that only realized profits may be recorded in the profit and loss account. However, realized is to be interpreted in the context of 'principles generally accepted' for accounting purposes. Thus, the rules of ACCOUNTING STANDARDS will normally determine what is deemed to be realized.

Also, UK company law requires that dividend distributions must not exceed accumulated realized profits less accumulated realized losses. Thus, profits and dividends cannot result from a plot of land that has been growing in value over many years, until the land is sold. There are similar provisions in the USA.

Receipts and payments account. For certain unincorporated enterprises, particularly those of a non-business or not-for-profit nature, conventional accounting, based on the MATCHING convention, may appear unnecessarily complicated. For them, a summary of cash amounts coming in or going out in a period may be sufficient. Such a summary would be called a receipts and payments account.

As an example of the differences between this and conventional accounting, consider the purchase of a new photocopying machine that is expected to last for ten years. Accountants would normally charge an amount of depreciation each year for the using up of the machine. However, a receipts and payments account would merely show the amount paid for the machine in the year that it was paid.

Not-for-profit organizations that are obliged to or wish to retain the MATCHING convention still produce income statements (US) or, in the UK, INCOME AND EXPENDITURE ACCOUNTS. These arrive at surpluses or deficits, rather than profits or losses.

Receivables. – the US expression for amounts of money due to a business, often known as ACCOUNTS RECEIVABLE. The UK term is 'debtors'.

Redeemable shares. – shares that may be bought back by the company that originally issued them. In the UK, most shares are not redeemable, whereas most loan stocks or debentures are. However, there is legal provision for shares to be made redeemable, and this is more normally used for preference shares.

The irredeemable nature of most UK shares is designed to protect creditors, by ensuring that a company cannot pay capital back to shareholders unless it is wound up, when all other claims would take priority. Thus when UK shares are allowed to be redeemed, the conditions are strict, and amounts have to be transferred from distributable profits to undistributable reserves (called capital redemption reserves).

Reducing balance depreciation. – a technique of calculating the depreciation charge, usually for machines, whereby the annual charge reduces over the years of an asset's life. A fixed percentage depreciation is charged each year on the cost (first year) or the undepreciated cost (subsequent years). There is a numerical illustration of this under the entry for DEPRECIATION.

The method is suitable for some machines that have increasing repair and maintenance expenses over their lives. The depreciation expense is designed gradually to fall, so that the total annual charge against profit for the use of the machine stays more or less static.

Registrar of Companies. – a UK government official who is charged with the collection, organization and granting of public access to the financial statements of companies. There are over 900,000 companies in the UK, so perhaps it is not surprising that many of them are allowed to escape without prompt filing (or without filing at all). The Registrar has no duty to examine the financial statements to ensure that they comply with detailed legal requirements.

This state of affairs may seem surprising to a US accountant who is used to the idea that companies registered with the SECURITIES AND EXCHANGE COMMISSION (including all listed companies) have their financial statements scrutinized much more carefully.

Regulation S-X. – an important source of rules relating to the preparation of financial statements for those companies registered with the SECURITIES AND EXCHANGE COMMISSION in the USA. For example, it is Regulation S-X that demands the inclusion of statements of changes in financial position (funds flow statements); and it also specifies detailed requirements for particular types of industry.

Relevant degrees. – academic degrees that allow entry into the training programmes or exemption from some parts of the examinations of various accountancy bodies. In some cases, the term 'qualifying degree' is used instead. Normally, such degrees contain financial accounting, management accounting, business finance, taxation, economics, law and statistics. Thus, some degrees that might be thought to be relevant for the work of an accountant, like a degree specializing in economics, will not be counted for this purpose.

Of course, the degree does not amount to a professional qualification. It merely qualifies the holder of the qualifying degree to enter training for the qualification!

'He came to us with a non-relevant degree and he's done nothing relevant ever since!'

Replacement cost accounting. – a system of preparing financial statements in which all assets (and expenses relating to them, like depreciation) are valued at current replacement costs. This is quite different from conventional accounting in which assets are normally valued at historical cost, which is simpler, more objective and easier to audit. However, replacement costs give much more up-to-date information about the value of assets and the costs of using them up. Under a replacement cost system, profits are calculated after deduction of a cost of sales and a depreciation charge based on the replacement cost of inventories and fixed assets.

The main example of a country where replacement cost accounting is used is the Netherlands. It is a minority practice there, and some companies have been publishing replacement cost financial statements for decades; for example, Philips since 1951. Some other companies produce notes to the financial statements about replacement costs.

In the UK and the USA, various systems of INFLATION ACCOUNTING have been proposed; some based on replacement costs. In the UK, in 1980, an accounting standard (SSAP 16) called for large and listed companies to publish supplementary (or main) financial statements based on current cost accounting, which normally uses replacement costs. In the USA, the accounting standard, SFAS 33, called for companies above a certain size to publish notes based on replacement cost and on general price level adjusted figures. Both standards were withdrawn as inflation rates fell.

Research and development. There has been controversy about how to account for R and D expenses. They are designed to bring benefit in future years, so it would seem unfair to charge all the expense this year (when there are no related revenues), and to recognize the revenues in a later year (when there are no related expenses). Thus, there is an argument for using the MATCHING principle here, and for treating the expenditure as an asset (capitalizing it), and only treating it as an expense in the future when the related revenues arrive.

Unfortunately, this goes against the principle of CONSERVATISM, because one can never be totally sure what (if any) the future revenues coming from present research and development will be.

In the USA, accounting standards (SFAS 2) demand that all R and D expenditure is charged immediately against profit. In the UK, this practice was also proposed. However, complaints from the aerospace industry led to the present standard (SSAP 13) allowing some development expenditure (but not research) to be capitalized under certain prudent conditions. Development expenditure may be distinguished because it has practical application to products or processes.

The financial collapse of Rolls Royce in the UK in the early 1970s was commonly held to be connected with excess capitalization of R and D expenditure. That was before SSAP 13 had been issued, and it should be more difficult for a company to follow such practices now.

Reserve recognition accounting (RRA). – a proposed system of accounting for oil and gas reserves by showing them on a basis linked to market values. The development of such a system was requested by the SECURITIES AND EXCHANGE COMMISSION in the USA in 1978, because they thought that the existing practice of valuing oil and gas at cost of exploration was very conservative (see OIL AND GAS ACCOUNTING).

However, the problems of arriving at an objective and reasonably prudent valuation method based on the size of reserves have been too difficult to resolve. Practice continues to be based on exploration costs in both the USA and the UK.

Reserves. – amounts notionally set aside out of profits (after the latter have been calculated), often to register the fact that they are voluntarily or compulsorily undistributable. Reserves should be distinguished from PROVISIONS. In the UK, the latter are charged in the calculation of profit, and represent reductions in the value of assets or anticipations of future liabilities. Of course, neither reserves nor provisions are amounts of cash. A provision is an accounting expense, and a reserve is an accounting allocation of undistributed profit from one heading to another. Reserves belong to shareholders, and are part of a total of shareholders' equity, which also includes share capital. This total is represented by all the assets of the business, less the liabilities owed to outsiders.

It should be noted that this terminology is used somewhat loosely by some accountants. For details of examples of PROVISIONS AND RESERVES, see the entry under that heading. In the USA, 'reserve' is used to cover some of the meanings of 'provision' in the UK.

Restricted surplus. – a US expression for amounts of past profit that are unavailable for distribution to shareholders. The UK equivalent would be 'undistributable reserves'.

Retained profit/earnings. – amounts of profit, earned in the preceding year and former years, that have not yet been paid out as dividends. 'Retained earnings' is a typical US expression for such amounts, though it would also be understood in the UK. 'Retained profit' is a more usual UK expression, although the formats required by the Companies Acts split up retained profits into a series of different RESERVES plus a general heading for the balance on the 'profit and loss account' (see Figure 2 under the entry for BALANCE SHEET).

Revaluation. Conventional accounting uses HISTORICAL COST as the basis for the valuation of assets. However, in some countries, including the UK but not the USA, it is acceptable to revalue fixed assets, either annually or from time to time. These revaluations can be done on the basis of current replacement cost or of NET REALIZABLE VALUE. It is quite normal for large UK companies to show land and buildings at revalued amounts in their balance sheets. Clearly, the purpose of this is to avoid a seriously misleading impression of their worth, when prices have risen substantially.

The problem with this permissive approach to valuation is that a reader of several sets of financial statements will be faced with a confusing mixture of historical costs and revaluations at various dates. It is essential to examine the notes to the balance sheet in order to discover how the fixed assets have been valued.

More consistent and extensive revaluation is to be found in various systems of INFLATION ACCOUNTING, such as that used for supplementary financial statements by large UK companies until 1985. Also, notes based on replacement costs are provided by large US companies.

Revenues. The revenues of an accounting period are those receipts of any period that relate to the accounting period. An analogous definition applies to expenses and payments. This is called the MATCHING or accruals convention.

For example, if an insurance company receives cash in 1985 for a 1986 insurance premium, the revenue will be recognized in 1986, not in the year of receipt. Similarly, when sales are made to customers 'on account' or 'on credit', those sales are recognized immediately, rather than waiting until the cash arrives.

Nearly all enterprises use the matching convention in this way, except for some of the smallest not-for-profit/non-business organizations that may use cash-based accounting for simplicity.

Revenue reserve. – a rather old-fashioned UK expression for amounts of retained profit that are available for distribution as dividends. In current UK balance sheets such an amount is found under the general heading 'capital and reserves', with a sub-heading of 'profit and loss account' (see Figure 2 under the entry for BALANCE SHEET). A similar US term would be unrestricted surplus.

Rights issue/offer. – the sale of additional shares by a company to its existing shareholders. The 'rights' to buy the shares, at slightly lower than the market price in order to ensure a full sale, are given out in proportion to the existing holdings. Thus, the existing group of shareholders may be largely preserved.

Since the sale is to existing shareholders, the advertisement and prospectus preparations need be far less expensive than for issues to the public. Thus, rights issues are cheaper and more popular than other means of selling new shares.

If a shareholder does not wish to take up the rights issue, he can sell the 'rights' because they enable another investor to purchase shares at a slight discount below the market price.

Rights issues should be distinguished from bonus/capitalization/scrip issues, where no money is paid to the company, but where existing shareholders receive a proportionate amount of free extra shares, and distributable profits are relabelled as share capital.

S

Sale-and-leaseback. – a method of raising funds by a company without immediately depleting resources or incurring liabilities. If a company owns and uses fixed assets, it may find it advantageous, for tax or other reasons, to sell them to a financial institution (the lessor) who then leases them back to the company.

The assets do not physically move as part of this process; so the company's business is not interrupted. The company receives a lump sum, which it may need for various purposes, and agrees to future lease payments. Legally, it no longer owns the assets, nor does it have a liability. However, since the real substance of the situation is not well represented by the legal form, it has now become accounting practice in the USA and the UK to record both an asset and a liability in the lessee's balance sheet (see LEASES).

Sales. The figure for sales recorded in the financial statements for a period will include all those sales agreed or delivered in the period, rather than those that are paid for in cash. The sales figure will be shown net of sales taxes (i.e. VAT in the UK).

In the UK, the word 'turnover' is used in the financial statements, although 'sales' is generally used in the books of account.

Companies are required to provide financial statement notes on the split of their sales by class of business and by geographical area of the world. These instructions are to be found in company law (UK)/accounting standard SFAS 14 (USA). This is called SEGMENTAL REPORTING.

Sandilands report. – the report of 1975 by the UK government committee on INFLATION ACCOUNTING chaired by Sir Francis Sandilands. It recommended that a system of CURRENT COST ACCOUNTING (CCA) be developed to take account of changing prices. Such a system is based mainly on current replacement costs. This is quite unlike the conventional HISTORICAL COST ACCOUNTING system that is still in use in most countries, or the general price level adjusted system of CURRENT PURCHASING POWER ACCOUNTING that the accountancy profession was recommending in the early 1970s.

It was not too surprising that the Sandilands Committee came to a different conclusion from the profession's rather simple method. A majority of the committee were not accountants, and most of the accountant minority were not typical. However, the profession reacted rapidly to produce an exposure draft for an accounting standard to be based on CCA. A decade of sometimes acrimonious debate has ensued (see CURRENT COST ACCOUNTING).

Scrip issue. A scrip, bonus or capitalization issue is made by a UK company to its existing shareholders in proportion to their shareholdings. The shareholders pay nothing for the issue. Instead, previously distributable profits are re-labelled as share capital and become undistributable. The purpose of this is sometimes to reduce the market price of the shares to a psychologically more appealing level. If there is a one for one bonus issue, the number of shares will double, followed presumably by a halving of the share price, other things being equal.

In the USA, such an issue may be either a STOCK DIVIDEND or a STOCK SPLIT.

Secret reserves. – various means by which a company, particularly a financial institution, can make its true financial strength unclear in its financial statements. The purpose of this is to build up resources in case of future difficulty. If that future difficulty eventually emerges, it may be possible to hide it completely by merely absorbing it with the secret reserves. This may avoid a dangerous loss of confidence in the bank or other company concerned.

Secret reserves may be created by deliberately allowing fixed assets or inventories (stocks) to be undervalued, or by creating unnecessary PROVISIONS.

The problem with such accounting practices is that they do indeed obscure the true financial position of a company from its shareholders and lenders. Thus, deliberate creation of secret reserves is not allowed for normal companies in the UK or the USA. However, the accounting practices of banks and insurance companies are somewhat mysterious, and are widely assumed to be very conservative. Secret reserves, especially large 'provisions for contingencies' are also common among all types of companies in continental Europe.

Of course, the conventional use of HISTORICAL COST ACCOUNTING normally implies some 'secret reserves' in the shape of land and buildings held at out-of-date costs.

Securities and Exchange Commission (SEC). – US government agency set up in 1934 after the Wall Street Crash of 1929. Its function is to control the issue and exchange of publicly traded shares. Companies with such shares must register with the SEC, and then obey a mass of detailed regulations about disclosure and audit of financial information. An SEC-registered company in the USA is the nearest equivalent to a public limited company in the UK. In both countries, not all such companies are listed on a stock exchange.

The SEC issues its own rules for financial reporting, such as Regulation S-X, which requires annual statements of changes in financial position and quarterly disclosure of sales and profit. Indeed, the only powerful requirements for disclosure and audit in the USA come from the SEC, directly or indirectly. The private body that sets accounting standards, the FINANCIAL ACCOUNTING STANDARDS BOARD, is given 'substantial authoritative support' by the SEC. However, the latter sometimes intervenes directly in the setting of accounting rules (see, for example, OIL AND GAS ACCOUNTING).

The form that must be sent annually by registered companies to the SEC is called the 10-K. This contains much accounting and economic information that supplements the published financial statements. The 10-K is available to the public.

Segmental reporting. – an analysis of sales or profit by line of business or by geographical area. Such reporting is required in the UK (by company law) and in the USA (by accounting standard SFAS 14). The purpose of segmental reporting is to enable the reader of financial statements to form a better view of the stability of the results of a company. For example, it may be useful to know what proportion of a company's sales and profits come from unstable African or Middle Eastern countries as opposed to those from Canada. It is these broad geographical segments that are envisaged, so companies with only one national market would fall outside the scope of the geographical rule. Similarly, a company that only operated supermarkets would only have one line of business.

In the USA, it is necessary to disclose revenue, operating profit and assets on a segmental basis. In the UK, sales and pre-tax profit should be disclosed for line-of-business segments, and only sales for geographical segments.

Shareholders' equity. – the total of the shareholders' interest in a company. This will include the original share capital, amounts contributed in excess of the PAR VALUE of shares (i.e. share premium or

Abbreviated Balance Sheet as at 31 December				
Land and Buildings		900	Ordinary Capital	1000
Plant		800	Share Premium	500
Vehicles		200	Profit and Loss	500
Total Fixed Assets		1900	*Shareholders' Equity*	2000
			Debenture Loans	1000
			Long-term Funds	3000
Stocks (inventory)	600			
Debtors	600			
Cash	400		Overdraft	200
Total Current Assets		1600	Creditors	300
			Total Current Liabilities	500
Total Assets		3500	*Total Capital and Liabs*	3500

paid-in surplus), and retained profits. In the USA, this total is sometimes called stockholders' equity.

For some measures of profitability, the annual EARNINGS of the company will be compared to the shareholders' equity.

The shareholders' equity will equal the NET ASSETS or net worth of the company. This is an inevitable result of the fact that a balance sheet balances, as illustrated on p. 150, with a two-sided balance sheet, using UK terms.

The net assets are the total assets less the liabilities. In this case, 3500 – 1000 – 500 = 2000. This is the same total as the shareholders' equity.

Share premium. – amounts paid into a company (by shareholders when they purchased shares from the company) in excess of the NOMINAL VALUE of the shares. The nominal value is little more than a label for the shares, but all UK shares have such a value. Shares are recorded at nominal values. However, share premium may be treated for most purposes exactly as if it were share capital. Both are included in SHARE-HOLDERS' EQUITY.

The US equivalent is 'paid-in surplus'.

Shares. – parts of the ownership of a company. Shareholders jointly own a company. In the case of most companies, the shareholders have limited liability for the company's debts. Thus, they are content to delegate the management of the company to boards of directors.

Most of the share capital of a company will have been provided by the holders of ORDINARY SHARES (UK)/COMMON STOCK (US). These shareholders can exercise their votes at the company's annual general meeting, when dividend decisions and much other business is done. They also share in the prosperity of the company because the dividends and the share value may be expected to rise over the years.

Shares are recorded in financial statements at their nominal or PAR VALUE, which distinguishes one type of share from another. Amounts paid in by shareholders who bought shares from the company at above par value are shown as share premium (UK)/paid-in surplus (US).

Shares are normally not redeemable by the company that issued them. However, most of the business of stock exchanges is done in the second-hand market for such securities.

See also PREFERENCE/PREFERRED SHARES, BONUS SHARES and RIGHTS ISSUES.

Société anonyme. – a French, Belgian, Luxembourg or Swiss public company. In continental Europe, most public companies are quite literally 'anonymous' because their shares are in 'bearer' form rather than being registered, as in the UK or the USA. This means that the shares can be legally transferred by being physically transferred. Thus, a company does not know who its owners are.

However, a majority of companies in France and the other countries above are in the private company form, that is the SOCIÉTÉ À RESPONSABILITÉ LIMITÉE.

Société à responsabilité limitée. – a French, Belgian, Luxembourg or Swiss private company. Such companies form the majority in these countries, just as private companies far outnumber public companies in the UK. The original design is the German *GmbH* form, which spread into France in 1925 when Alsace and Lorraine became French again.

The *Sàrl* is not exactly like a UK private company. For example, its shares are similar to partnership shares.

Solvency. A business (or person) is solvent if it can pay its bills or accounts as they fall due. The likely ability of a business to do this can be measured by examining its LIQUIDITY.

Source and application of funds. Statements of source and application of funds are required as part of the financial statements of companies in the UK and the USA. They are also known as funds flow statements and, in the USA, as statements of changes in financial position. They are designed to concentrate on flows of funds, rather than flows of revenues or expenses as in profit and loss accounts (UK)/income statements (US). Revenues and expenses are calculated using the MATCHING concept that deliberately avoids using the cash basis.

Thus, for example, when a plot of land is purchased for cash, no effect will be shown in a profit and loss account, because the land is treated as an asset. In a funds flow statement, however, the full purchase price will be shown as a use of funds for the period.

In the UK, the rules for this type of statement are to be found in an accounting standard (SSAP 10), which exempts companies with an annual turnover below £25,000. In the USA, the requirement is to be found in REGULATION S-X of the Securities and Exchange Commission. It thus applies with particular force to SEC-registered companies.

In both countries, the statements are to be based on CONSOLIDATED FINANCIAL STATEMENTS and are to be audited. They should contain a minimum of netting off of inflows against outflows. For example, sales of plant should not be netted off against purchases of plant.

SSAP. – an abbreviation for Statement of Standard Accounting Practice, that is an ACCOUNTING STANDARD of the UK and Ireland.

Stag. – a speculator on a stock exchange who buys newly issued securities in advance at a fixed price, presuming that there will be a shortage of them so that he can rapidly sell when the price rises. See, also, BEAR and BULL.

Standards. See ACCOUNTING STANDARDS and AUDITING STANDARDS.

Statement of changes in financial position. – the US expression for the annual financial statement that concentrates on the flows of funds in a company during the accounting period. In the UK, these are called funds flow statements or SOURCE AND APPLICATION OF FUNDS statements. See that entry for more details.

Statements of financial accounting concepts. – statements from the US Financial Accounting Standards Board; issued as part of the search for a CONCEPTUAL FRAMEWORK. They deal with such matters as the objectives and elements of financial statements.

Statements of financial accounting standards (SFAS). – the US term for ACCOUNTING STANDARDS as set by the Financial Accounting Standards Board since its foundation in 1973. These are the technical rules of valuation, measurement and disclosure for financial statements.

Statements of recommended practice (SORPs). – guidance, issued by the ACCOUNTING STANDARDS COMMITTEE (ASC) in the UK, with less authority than accounting standards. They are designed to deal with particular industries or with specialist technical problems. In cases where the contents have been drafted by an industry or special interest group and then sent to the ASC for approval, the result will be a 'franked SORP'.

Statements of standard accounting practice (SSAPs). – the UK term for ACCOUNTING STANDARDS, as set by the Accounting Standards Committee since its foundation in 1970. These are the technical rules of valuation, measurement and disclosure for financial statements. They supplement the rules to be found in Companies Acts, though they are less authoritative. See ACCOUNTING STANDARDS for more details.

Stewardship. – the original purpose of accounting; also called 'accountability'. Kings or lords who were away at war or for other purposes would leave their estates in the hands of a steward. The steward would keep an account of the payments and receipts of the estate so that he could be discharged of responsibility when the owner returned. The steward would 'render an account' to the owner, who might have been illiterate and had thus to hear it ('audit' is Latin for 'he hears').

Today, shareholders are the owners of companies, and directors are their appointees who look after the assets in their absence. Thus, the annual financial statements need to be checked by independent experts (the auditors) and sent to the shareholders. Thus it may be seen whether the directors have been proper stewards.

In recent years, the financial statements have come to be seen as provision of information useful for taking decisions about whether to buy or sell a company's securities. This requires forward-looking information, whereas stewardship is essentially backward-looking. This conflict had led to difficulties in setting rules for, and in interpreting, financial statements. For example, it could be claimed that HISTORICAL COST ACCOUNTING was more useful for stewardship than for financial decision-making.

Stock. – US term for securities of various kinds; for example, COMMON STOCK or PREFERENCE STOCK (equivalent to ordinary and preference shares in UK terminology). However, the word 'share' is also understood in the USA, so that 'stockholder' and 'shareholder' are interchangeable.

In the UK this meaning survives, particularly in the expressions 'Stock Exchange' and 'Loan Stock'.

A source of great confusion in Anglo-American conversation is the UK use of the word 'stocks' for what are called inventories in the USA.

Stock dividend/stock split. – US terms to describe the issue of free extra shares to existing shareholders, combined with the capitalization of retained earnings. A stock dividend is an extra issue of up to about 25 per cent of the number of existing shares. A stock split is an extra issue of over about 20 per cent. The two issues are accounted for differently.

The UK equivalent expressions are bonus/scrip/capitalization issues.

Stock exchange. – an organized market for the issue of new securities and the exchange of second-hand ones. Companies whose shares may be sold on such exchanges are called listed or quoted companies. They must be public companies (for the UK) or registered with the SECURITIES AND EXCHANGE COMMISSION (for the USA). In addition to the normal accounting regulations, listed companies have to obey the 'listing requirements' of their particular Stock Exchange. Such requirements may include extra disclosure of accounting data or of facts concerning their executives or their plans. In the UK, it is the listing requirements of the London Stock Exchange that call for half-yearly 'interim' financial information.

The largest and most active exchanges in the world are those of

London and New York. The international differences in the number of domestic listed companies are quite remarkable, and are illustrated below with recent approximate figures:

London	2217
New York S.E.	1500
American	774
W Germany (all)	442
Paris	736
Amsterdam	215
Milan	130

Stock relief. – a UK tax relief that operated between 1973 and 1984. It was designed to allow for the fact that reported profits included gains on the holding of inventories/stocks that were merely due to price increases. Businesses had to maintain these higher value inventories, which meant that the gains could not be used to pay tax.

Stockholders' equity. – US expression for the total stake in a company owned by the stockholders, including their invested capital and retained earnings. A more detailed entry may be found under SHAREHOLDERS' EQUITY, which is an expression also used in the USA, and more readily understood in the UK.

Stocks. As used in the UK, this word means the raw materials, work-in-progress and finished goods of a business. Unfortunately, in the USA the word means shares (see STOCK). Thus, this book uses the more readily understood international term, INVENTORIES, for what are usually known as stocks in the UK (see that entry for more details).

Stock split. – see STOCK DIVIDEND.

Straight-line depreciation. – a system of calculating the annual depreciation expense of a fixed asset. This method charges equal annual instalments against profit over the useful life of the asset. In total, the cost of the asset less any estimated scrap value is depreciated. This method is simple to use and thus very popular.

For a numerical illustration and a description of alternative methods, see DEPRECIATION.

Subsidiary. – generally, a company, more than half of whose shares are owned by another company (the parent company). The accounting treatment is to prepare CONSOLIDATED FINANCIAL STATEMENTS that include the parent company and all its subsidiaries.

Substance over form. – the presentation in financial statements of the real economic substance of a particular transaction, rather than the legal or technical form of it. This is an underlying idea in the world of ANGLO-SAXON ACCOUNTING. For example, when plant is leased by a lessee from a lessor there is no transfer of legal ownership or creating of legal liabilities. However, in many cases, the transaction is very similar to a purchase of assets and borrowing of money by the lessee. The plant will be at the lessee's premises, and the lessee will have contracted to pay a series of future lease payments. To concentrate on the legal form of the transaction would ignore the economic reality. Thus, it is gradually becoming practice for accountants in the Anglo-Saxon world to capitalize leases and future lease payments (see LEASES).

This method of thinking is taken the furthest in the USA. Another example there is the notional correction of interest receipts or payments on loans which have a non-commercial rate of interest.

T

Table A. – a model set of ARTICLES OF ASSOCIATION, to be found in the UK Companies Acts. The Articles of a company are the rules that govern the relationships among shareholders, and between shareholders and the company and its directors. A company in the process of formation may adopt or amend Table A for its own purposes.

T-account. – see ACCOUNTS.

Tangible assets. – assets with physical existence, like property, plant or equipment. Normally this term is not extended to physical current assets, like inventory/stocks. Tangible assets may be contrasted with investments and with INTANGIBLE ASSETS, like patents, trademarks or goodwill.

Taxable income. – annual business net income, as adjusted from accounting rules to tax rules. In the UK in particular, there are numerous adjustments from accounting net profit to taxable income. For example, accounting depreciation is added back, and CAPITAL ALLOWANCES are granted instead. Dividend income from other companies is deducted, but certain legal fees and entertainment expenses are added back. For more details, see CORPORATION TAX.

Temporal method. – the principal method of FOREIGN CURRENCY TRANSLATION used in the USA between 1975 and 1981. It is now only to be used in particular circumstances.

10-K report. – an annual report required by the SECURITIES AND EXCHANGE COMMISSION of the USA to be delivered by all companies registered with it. The Form 10-K contains many detailed disclosures of an accounting and statistical nature, concerning executives, share issues and so on. Some of the information is similar to that required in Directors' Reports in the UK.

Times covered/times interest earned. – ratios that measure the security of a company's future dividends, interest payments or profits. The 'times covered' or 'dividend cover' normally refers to the number of times that the company's most recent total annual dividends could have been paid out of its annual EARNINGS available for that purpose. A low cover suggests that future dividends may be in doubt if the company suffers any setback.

The 'times interest earned' ratio compares the most recent annual interest payments of a company with its net profit before interest and tax, which is available for such interest payments. Again, if the cover is low, the company may be in danger of not being able to make future interest payments. This might lead to its being compulsorily wound up.

Timing difference. – a difference in the accounting year when certain expenses are charged in the calculation of profit as opposed to the year when allowed as deductions in the calculation of taxable income. For example, accelerated depreciation for tax purposes (capital allowances, in the UK) will allow plant and machinery to be charged for tax purposes over a shorter period than that used by accountants as the useful life for depreciation in financial statements.

Such timing differences may lead to the need to account for DEFERRED TAX.

Trade creditors. – suppliers of goods or services to the business, who are not paid immediately at the time of purchase. At a balance sheet date, outstanding amounts owed to them will be shown as 'trade creditors' as part of current liabilities.

Trade marks. – names or designs that a business has a right to use in connection with its products. Accountants will put a value on these for balance sheet purposes only if that 'value' can be verified because the trade mark was bought or was created using separately identifiable expenses. Thus, the value of a trade mark will be recorded as its cost.

Trade marks are examples of INTANGIBLE ASSETS, like patents or goodwill.

Transfer pricing. – the notional or real price charged by one part of a company (or group of companies) to another part when goods or services are transferred. Setting low transfer prices shifts profits to the receiver of the goods; setting high transfer prices shifts profits to the producer. The implications for the management of divisionalized or multinational companies are very great: 'wrong' prices lead to 'wrong' profits.

When there is more than one country involved, transfer prices become important as a means of moving profits around the world for political, exchange control or tax reasons.

Treasury stock. – US expression for a company's shares that have been bought back by the company and not cancelled. The shares are held 'in the corporate treasury'. They receive no dividends and carry no votes at company meetings.

The UK equivalent term is 'own shares'. The term 'treasury stock' is confusing to a UK reader because it might appear to refer to government bonds.

Trial balance. – part of the exercise of producing financial statements from the records in a DOUBLE ENTRY bookkeeping system. The trial balance marshals all the debit and credit balances on the various accounts on to one page. If the recording of double entries has been done correctly throughout the preceding period, the total of debits should equal the total of credits. If it does not, the errors must be found before correct financial statements can be prepared.

From a trial balance, all the revenue and expense balances are taken to create a profit and loss account (UK)/income statement (US). The balance on this, plus all the remaining balances on the trial balance (assets, liabilities and capital) are used to create the BALANCE SHEET.

True and fair view. – the overriding legal requirement for the presentation of financial statements of companies in the UK and most of the Commonwealth. The US equivalent is 'fair presentation'. It is difficult to tie down an exact meaning to the expression, and it would ultimately have to be interpreted in a court of law. However, the law demands *a* true and fair view, rather than *the* true and fair view; and it is clear that the instruction has to be interpreted in the context of normal accounting practice at the time of the financial statements.

In the UK, the law requires that extra information must be disclosed if this is necessary to give a true and fair view. In extreme cases, detailed provisions of the law may be departed from if this is the only way of giving a true and fair view. In such cases, there must be disclosure of the reasons and effects of the departures (see INVESTMENT PROPERTIES).

'You've certified that in your view their accounts are 'fairly true'!'

The UK was successful in inserting the overriding requirement for a true and fair view into the EEC's FOURTH DIRECTIVE on company law. This harmonizing measure is gradually being enacted throughout the EEC's member states. Thus, for example, French financial statements must now present an *image fidèle*. However, it seems clear that this requirement will not lead to such flexibility as is common in the UK.

Turnover. – the UK expression used in profit and loss accounts for the sales revenue of an accounting period. This is shown net of value added tax.

Companies are required to provide financial statement notes on the split of their turnover by line of business and by geographical area. This is called SEGMENTAL REPORTING.

U

Ultra vires. – latin expression for 'beyond the powers'. An action of a company or a director is *ultra vires* if it is beyond the legal powers of the company (as set out in the MEMORANDUM OF ASSOCIATION) or the director (as set out in the ARTICLES OF ASSOCIATION or in Companies Acts). Such actions may, for example, lead to contracts being void.

Underwriting expenses. – costs incurred when a company engages a financial institution to 'underwrite' a new issue of shares. The underwriter agrees to take up any unsold shares at a specified price. This is one of the many costs of share issues, along with banking advice, legal fees and advertising. Such costs have to be treated as expenses of the year of issue; they must not be capitalized (treated as assets).

Undistributable reserves. – amounts, paid in by shareholders or notionally allocated out of profits, that are not available for distribution to the shareholders as dividends. The US term is 'restricted surplus'.

Undistributable reserves would include SHARE PREMIUM (UK)/PAID-IN SURPLUS (US) and reserves on the revaluation of assets. See, also, DISTRIBUTABLE PROFITS.

Uniformity. – the use of the same rules of accounting or financial statement presentation from one company to another. Improvements in uniformity are encouraged by the setting of ACCOUNTING STANDARDS. One reason for this is to improve comparability between the financial statements of different companies.

The word 'consistency' tends to be used for the use by any individual company of the same accounting methods year by year. This is required by company law.

Unit Trusts. – financial institutions whose main aim is to use the money provided by their investors in order to own and manage profitably a portfolio of investments in other stocks and shares. Unlike INVESTMENT TRUSTS, they are 'open-ended funds' in that their investors will be constantly contributing and withdrawing cash by buying and selling units in the trust. The equivalent US term is 'mutual fund'.

Unlimited company. – a UK legal entity, in the form of a company, whose shareholders do not have LIMITED LIABILITY for the debts of the company. Such companies are fairly rare, but they do have the advantage that some provisions of company law do not apply, including the requirement to publish financial statements.

Unsecured loan stock. – loan securities that are not specifically guaranteed by mortgaged assets of the borrower company. In the event of the company not being able to pay the interest or to repay the capital at the redemption date, the holders of the securities would petition a court for the winding up of the company. They would be behind the secured creditors in order of payment, because the proceeds of the sale of the mortgaged assets would be available for the latter. However, their claims would be settled before those of the shareholders.

The word 'debenture' is not normally used for unsecured loan stock.

V

Value added statements. – supplementary financial statements prepared by some UK companies. They rearrange, and may add to, the information provided in a profit and loss account. The statement begins with a calculation of a measure of total output: sales, additions to inventories/stocks, other incomes, and fixed assets created by the business for its own use. Then the statements show deductions from this: amounts paid to suppliers of goods and services, amounts paid to employees, depreciation, interest, taxation, and dividends. It may be seen as useful propaganda by some companies to show what a large proportion of the output goes to employees and the government, and what a small proportion to shareholders.

Value added statements are increasing in popularity but are still fairly rare in the UK, and even rarer elsewhere. They were recommended in a document from the UK's Accounting Standards Committee in 1975: *The Corporate Report*.

Value for money audit (VFM). – investigations of the efficiency of use of resources by organizations whose main aim is not profit. The accountability of some such bodies is very poor; they may have no owners, multiple objectives and no clear measures of success.

In the UK in the 1980s, there have been considerable efforts to develop VFM audits for local government and other public concerns.

Value to the business. – a basis on which to value assets, used as part of some systems of INFLATION ACCOUNTING; also called 'value to the owner'. The valuation of an asset would be based on the concept of

'If you can program it to capitalise the cost of computer software at its value to the business, you'll be worth your weight in gold, Pauline'

DEPRIVAL VALUE, whereby an asset is deemed to be worth the amount by which the business would be worse off without it. For most assets owned by a going concern, the deprival value would be the net current replacement cost; that is, the amount that it would now cost to buy a replacement, less an adjustment for the degree to which the asset is worn out. However, under some circumstances, net realizable value or economic value would be used (see DEPRIVAL VALUE).

Variable costs. – costs that vary in proportion to the volume of production. Normally, raw materials and direct labour input will be variable costs. Some overhead costs, that cannot be directly ascribed to particular units of production or processes, may nevertheless still be variable with total production.

Variable costs are sometimes called MARGINAL COSTS by accountants. The opposite of these are fixed costs, that do not vary in the short term over the range of production levels being considered. For some decision-making purposes it will be useful to consider only the variable costs and variable revenues of competing possibilities. A problem for this is that many costs appear to be semi-variable, unless much investigation or estimation is carried out.

Variances. – differences between actual amounts of costs, revenues, production levels, etc and the plans for those amounts set down in BUDGETS.

The planning process involved in setting budgets may be useful *per se*, but budgetary control really becomes a powerful system when variances are reported frequently and promptly, and when correct action is taken by managers as a result.

Calculating variances can be complex, because the causes of a difference between actual and budgeted production expenses, for example, may be variances in prices, product mix, volume of production, and so on. Variance analysis splits down the differences into these various causes so that managers know where to direct their attention.

Vredeling Directive. – a draft DIRECTIVE OF THE EEC on company law, first drafted by the EEC Commission at the behest of a former Commissioner, named Vredeling. It concerns the giving of information to employees, and the involvement of the latter in the decision-making of larger companies. At the time of writing, the latest EEC document is the draft of 1983. The UK's Conservative Government is opposed to the Directive.

W

Weighted average cost. – a method of determining the cost of INVEN-
TORIES/stocks that are on hand at the end of an accounting period, in
those normal cases where it is either difficult or impossible to determine
exactly which units remain. If a business buys and uses many types of
raw materials, it may be hard to tell which units have been used and
which remain; and thus difficult to calculate the exact costs. Thus, it is
normal to make flow assumptions like first in, first out (FIFO) or last
in, first out (LIFO) or average cost.

   'Weighted average cost' values units used and units remaining at the
average cost of the purchases, weighted by volume. The average may be
worked out each time there is another purchase, or at pre-determined
intervals.

West Germany. Financial reporting by West German companies is substantially different from that in the UK or the USA. Until recently,
only the relatively small number of public companies (AG) and some
large private companies (GmbH) had to produce audited and published
financial statements. Further, the preparation of CONSOLIDATED
FINANCIAL STATEMENTS was restricted to such companies, and only had
to include West German subsidiaries. It is also commonly held that
German accounting is far more conservative than Anglo-American accounting, and that it is more concerned with legal correctness than with
fairness of presentation.

   In 1985, the fourth, seventh and eighth DIRECTIVES OF THE EEC
were implemented in West Germany, with various effective dates from
1987 year-ends onwards. When fully in force, the new laws will entail
a great extension of audit and publication for private companies. The
TRUE AND FAIR VIEW is also introduced, at least in name. Consolidation
along Anglo-American lines will also become the norm for all but small
groups. The German accounting profession is well organized and its
members are highly qualified. However, it is small, weak and young
compared to its Anglo-American counterparts (see Institut der
Wirtschaftsprüfer in the table under ACCOUNTANCY PROFESSION).

Winding-up. – the legal procedures for the termination of a company.

Window dressing. – the manipulation of figures in financial statements
in order to make them appear better (or perhaps worse) than they otherwise would be. A company might wish to do this in order to affect the
actions of existing or potential shareholders or lenders, the government,
or other readers of financial statements.

   It would, of course, be possible for a company totally to invent
assets, to ignore liabilities, to understate expenses or to exaggerate
revenues. Many such manouevres should be discovered by auditors.

However, window dressing is normally more subtle. It rests upon the fact that there are competing conventions and choices of practices in accounting. Where extensive judgement is used, extensive manipulation is a possibility.

One of the principles of accounting that should control this is CON-SISTENCY. For example, once a method of depreciation has been chosen, it should be maintained throughout an asset's life. Unfortunately, particularly in UK accounting, there is ample opportunity for inconsistency; for example, in the valuation of assets. Also, there is room for manoeuvre in such matters as DEFERRED TAX and DEVELOPMENT EXPENDITURE.

In both the UK and the USA, the valuation of inventories/stocks or the estimation of provisions/allowances for doubtful debts leaves considerable room for the exercise of judgement. In many cases, the action of making this year look better will make a future year look worse. However, some manipulations may bring 'benefit' for many years. A reader of financial statements will be able to see through some of these adjustments by careful reading of the notes to the financial statements.

See, also, CREATIVE ACCOUNTING.

Working capital. – the difference between current assets and current liabilities. This total is also known as NET CURRENT ASSETS, under which entry there are more details.

Work-in-progress. – partially manufactured goods, on their way from being raw materials to being finished products. Such goods are included in INVENTORIES/stocks, and are usually valued at the various costs involved in their production.

Writing-down allowances. – annual depreciation of FIXED ASSETS for tax purposes in the UK. The allowances form part of the CAPITAL ALLOWANCES system. For cars, the WDA is 25 per cent using the reducing balance method; for industrial buildings, it is 4 per cent on a straight-line basis. From 1 April, 1986 the capital allowances system will change, such that plant and machinery will also receive 25 per cent WDAs.

Written-down value. – amount at which assets are usually held in books of account and in financial statements. This is the historical cost less an allowance for wearing out, called ACCUMULATED DEPRECIATION. The expression 'net book value' has the same meaning.

The same expression may also be used for the amount of an asset that has not yet been allowed as depreciation for tax purposes; this would be the tax written-down value.

Y

Yield. The earnings yield or the dividend yield of an ordinary (UK)/common (US) share is the latest annual EARNINGS or dividend as a proportion of the market price of the share.

Z

Zero-base budgeting. – a system of budgeting originally developed in the USA for enterprises facing rapid changes in technology and sales. The system involves a more radical starting from scratch each year than the traditional system of BUDGETS does. Managers must justify their activities as though they were being started for the first time.

Z-score. – a measure of the likelihood of a business becoming insolvent. It uses a combination of commonly used RATIOS. The combination has been calculated by studying the ratios of businesses that have failed in the past.

Abbreviations

Here are some of the abbreviations commonly used by accountants. In many cases there are entries for them in the main text, usually under the unabbreviated expression.

AAA	American Accounting Association
ACA	Associate of the Institute of Chartered Accountants in England and Wales
ACCA	Associate of the Chartered Association of Certified Accountants
ACMA	Associate of the Chartered Institute of Management Accountants
ACT	advance corporation tax (UK)
AG	Aktiengesellschaft (German or Swiss public company)
AGM	annual general meeting
AICPA	American Institute of Certified Public Accountants
AISG	Accountants International Study Group
APB	Accounting Principles Board
APC	Auditing Practices Committee (UK)
ARB	Accounting Research Bulletin
ARS	Accounting Research Study
ASC	Accounting Standards Committee (UK)
ASR	Accounting Series Release of the SEC
CA	Chartered accountant
CACA	Chartered Association of Certified Accountants
CAPM	capital asset pricing model
CCA	current cost accounting
CCAB	Consultative Committee of Accountancy Bodies (UK and Ireland)
CGT	capital gains tax
CICA	Canadian Institute of Chartered Accountants
CIMA	Chartered Institute of Management Accountants
CIPFA	Chartered Institute of Public Finance and Accountancy
COB	Commission des opérations de bourse (Stock Exchange Commission, France)

CONSOB	Commissione nazionale per le società e la borsa (Stock Exchange Commission, Italy)
COSA	cost of sales adjustment
CPA	certified public accountant
CPP	current purchasing power accounting
CRC	current replacement cost
cr	credit (in double entry bookkeeping)
CTT	capital transfer tax
CVP	cost-volume-profit analysis
DCF	discounted cash flow
dr	debit (in double entry bookkeeping)
EBIT	earnings before interest and tax
ECU	European currency unit
EDP	electronic data processing
EEC	European Economic Community
EFT	electronic funds transfer
EFTPOS	electronic funds transfer at the point of sale
EOQ	economic order quantity
EPS	earnings per share
EV	economic value
FASB	Financial Accounting Standards Board (USA)
FCA	Fellow of the Institute of Chartered Accountants in England and Wales
FCCA	Fellow of the Chartered Association of Certified Accountants
FCMA	Fellow of the Chartered Institute of Management Accountants
FEE	Federation des experts comptables européens
FIFO	first in, first out
FII	franked investment income
GAAP	generally accepted accounting principles
GAAS	generally accepted auditing standards
GAS	Government Accounting Service (UK)
GASB	Governmental Accounting Standards Board (USA)
GmbH	Gesellschaft mit beschränkter Haftung (German or Swiss private company)
IASC	International Accounting Standards Committee
ICAEW	Institute of Chartered Accountants in England and Wales
ICAI	Institute of Chartered Accountants in Ireland
ICAS	Institute of Chartered Accountants of Scotland
ICCAP	International Coordination Committee for the Accounting Profession
IFAC	International Federation of Accountants
IRR	internal rate of return

IRS	Internal Revenue Service (USA)
LIFO	last in, first out
MCT	mainstream corporation tax
MWCA	monetary working capital adjustment
NPV	net present value
NRV	net realizable value
P/E	price/earnings ratio
P & L a/c	profit and loss account
PLC or plc	public limited company (UK)
PRT	petroleum revenue tax (UK)
R & D	research and development
ROCE	return on capital employed
ROI	return on investment
RRA	reserve recognition accounting (for oil and gas)
SA	société anonyme (French, Belgian, Luxembourg or Swiss public company)
Sàrl	Société à responsabilité limitée (French, etc private company)
SEC	Securities and Exchange Commission (USA)
SFAC	Statement of Financial Accounting Concepts (USA)
SFAS	Statement of Financial Accounting Standards (USA)
SORP	Statement of Recommended Practice (UK)
SSAP	Statement of Standard Accounting Practice (UK)
TB	trial balance
UEC	Union Européenne des Experts Comptables Economiques et Financiers
USM	Unlisted Securities Market (UK)
VAT	value added tax
VFM	value for money
WDV	written down value
ZBB	zero base budgeting